REQUIEM FOR WARRIORS

A novel

by

Norman Weissman

In Loving Memory of:
Herbert Lerner USAF
Robert Nassau USAF
Sol Tyson USA
1925 -1945

Copyright © 2020 by Norman Weissman

All Rights reserved under International and Pan American Copyright Convention

Published in the United States by Hammonasset House Books, Clinton, CT

Cataloging-in-Publication Data is available from

Library of Congress

History/Fiction

ISBN 978-0-9966-169-4-2

FICO: 14000

www.HammonassetHouse.com

Printed in the United States of America

Book Distribution by Ingram

Cover by Lee Jacobus

"*Requiem for Warriors* is a tribute to three of author Norman Weissman's high school classmates who died in a combat during World war II. Weissman, a Navy pilot during the war, portrays his friend's lives and deaths in the "good" war with remarkable fidelity to who they were as individuals and how and where they died, before shifting to a tale about how several generations of fictional warriors were affected by this war. These warriors—German, French, and English—warriors for hire who sacrificed their souls fighting wars to protect the colonial interests of declining European powers against native populations seeking freedom in the aftermath of World War II and beyond. Weissman brings his considerable knowledge of history to the story of their struggle to find meaning, if not redemption, for their own horrific actions in the name of patriotism and ideologies that have led nations to self-destruction. What makes this story so compelling is that all of these warriors, including the "good guys," were guilty of crimes against humanity, prompted by beliefs justifying their inhumane actions. "Requiem" is about the pity of war, about how war corrupts a nation's values of right and wrong, "creating societies where conformity becomes a virtue, dissent a crime." Everyone, says one lover of a warrior from an enemy country, "fights their own war. We are all warriors." The underlying question that haunts Weissman's tale is: "Can a good man do evil?" We are beginning to find an answer to this question as we begin to question the values of the very founders who uniquely defined the idea of America. Recognizing our own complicity in inhuman actions is vital to our survival as a moral and just society. This is the admonition of History; it is the heart and soul of Weissman's *Requiem*."

Larry Dowler Ph.D.
Archivist Yale University (1970-1982)
Librarian, Widener Library
Harvard University (1982-1998)

"Requiem For Warriors dramatizes the sacrifice of patriots fighting to prevent democracy from descending into a dark age where civilizations self-destruct by breaking faith with their fundamental values. Norman Weissman presents an overview of a changing world that seems beyond control by international institution, an important book."

>Myles Gansfried
>Playwright Author of:
>"Once Upon a Park Bench"
>"The Computer Lesson"

"Skillfully weaving together a tapestry of lives, loves, history and ideas, Norman Weissman presents us with the drama of our turbulent times challenging us to examine the basic conflicts and paradoxes thinking people must confront."

>Ammi Kohn
>Author of "Lama Genesis, Lama Incarnations"

Also by Norman Weissman

The Patriot
The Prodigy
Oh Palestine!
Snapshots USA
Acceptable Losses
Prospect Park Stories
My Exuberant Voyage

PROLOGUE

I write with fidelity to the truth I have witnessed as my imagination pursues the facts of history. I show what happened to friends who live on in my mind questioning the mysteries of Life, death and time. I speak of remarkable lives describing how wars overturn civilizations, corrupting concepts of right and wrong, and how, ignoring consequences, people panic dooming nations to self-destruct. I warn brutality, evoked by intolerance and fear, corrupts a nation's values creating societies where conformity becomes a virtue, dissent a crime.

My subject is War -- and the pity of War.

ONE

One weekend, in 1960, when working for BBC London, I drove to the American Military Cemetery in Cambridge to say Kaddish for my High School classmate Herbert Lerner. In 1943 returning from his 22nd Bombing Mission, his B-17 crash landed in England killing all onboard. With two burned out engines, flying on a wing and a prayer, their final approach to the runway obscured by fog, they flew into the ground, exploded and burned adding nine more casualties to the 8th Air Force's total of 89,000 young American Aviators.

Driving past England' carefully cultivated farms, hedges and hay stacks, with ancient trees wearing the first green harbingers of Spring, my mournful feelings vanished as I escaped crowded London sharing the Poet's joy writing 'about the woodland I will go to see the cherry hung with snow.'

Searching for A Star of David amid rows of white crosses led me to Herb's grave identified by name, rank, date of birth and death. After reciting the prayer for the dead, placing a remembrance stone on his grave, I thought about Herb's fatal flight returning to England after creating a Firestorm of death and destruction over Dresden. A loss of oil pressure overheated two engines with flames and wildly rotating propellers threatening to destroy their bomber they dove down in a desperate attempt to extinguish the flames. With only two working engines they fought to stay aloft, throwing overboard machine guns, ammunition boxes, radios, and parachutes losing altitude as they flew over Germany and France shouting joyfully as they crossed the English channel five hundred feet above a sea that would drown them all. England's early morning Fogs were an enemy they could not vanquish. Relentless Pea-soup Fogs clouded England as far inland as Wales. Flying blind, without a horizon for orientation, Herb Lerner descended through the overcast praying to see the ground before crashing.

As a High School Senior, Herb Lerner was the life of every party. Our monthly Amateur Hour in the school's auditorium included singers, Tap dancers, Magicians, Guitar and Banjo players and aspiring violin Prodigies of limited talent and skill. Herb calmly delivered his monologues and pantomimes, pretending surprise as he ignited waves of laughter. Bob Hope was his role model, and when Herb Lerner ended his performance singing 'Thanks for the memory' -- adolescent girls cried hysterically. Our Senior Year Book predicted a brilliant future for Herb as a Star of stage and screen.

A bombing mission over Germany was not a high school Amateur Hour. I imagined Herb's anxious hours flying to targets with his Brooklyn accented voice joking and singing on the intercom -- 'Off we go into the Wild Blue Yonder' -- or -- 'I'll take the Dames -- let my Buddies go down in Flames' -- ignoring orders to maintain Radio silence. Herb worked hard dispelling the contagion of fear in the air they breathed -- banishing feelings they were children lost amidst the dark horrors of skies blackened by exploding Flack.

Herb sang -- 'I've had a bellyful of war' -- as their B 17 rocked and rolled with the shock waves of exploding anti-aircraft fire. Returning to England, Herb shouted triumphantly -- 'We're too young to die in this fucking German sky!' -- remaining silent on the long flight returning to crowded English Pubs serving Pints of Beer raucously singing -- 'the Bells of Hell go ting- a ling – a ling – for you but not for me!' -- confirming the miracle they were alive. Greeted by shouts of -- 'over paid, over sexed, and over here' -- American G.I.'s drinking in crowded Pubs when called 'Bloody Yanks', raised their Beer mugs, saluting English soldiers who did not conceal their envy of the 'Yanks' greater popularity with English girls.

"And it's true," Kati Pollard told me, "Americans have beautiful smiles and attractive teeth and they know how to date a girl as if she were a young lady inviting her to a movie or a dinner when they come to town. Respectable girls do not drink alone in Pubs and I liked being with Herb and how he treated me even though I was too thin, had pale skin and kinky hair. Years of austerity rations made me look like an emaciated survivor of the 'Blitz' that seemed to never end. A good hot meal was most welcome even when interrupted by German Missiles.

Every morning at dawn, I heard the roar and rumble of B-17s starting engines and taking off from a nearby Airfield, circling overhead as they joined-up in large formations departing for Europe. Then, because my dear Herb was flying there would be a very long day, counting hours, waiting for the reassuring sound of returning squadrons now reduced in number followed by the welcome relief of Herb's phone call inviting me to dinner. After several weeks of excruciating worry I realized I was madly in love with Herb Lerner from Brooklyn New York in the good old USA.

My daily routine consisted of working at our village's Bakery selling bread and Scones and cookies, with anxious afternoons waiting for Herb's blessed voice and praying for his safe return. I was not the only woman waiting for husbands, sons and lovers to return from the war. Wives, girlfriends and mothers did their shopping, tended gardens, accompanied their children to school their worried faces reflecting courage and optimism. 'England can take it' was more than a slogan but a fact I witnessed every day when customers gave me their ration coupons with trembling hands and brave smiles. Our school's Children's Chorus, singing with breaking adolescent voices -- 'There will always be an England and England will be free' expressed our country's undaunted Patriotism. Yes! -- Yes! -- it was good to be alive and when Herb was not flying we rode our bicycles through the beautiful English countryside, two children playing in a world without war. Spreading a blanket under an old Oak tree at the crest of a hill near our village, we ate a picnic lunch and sipped wine thinking about peaceful years with promises of our future as we slowly, tenderly, made love.

I first saw herb when he entered our shop. walked to the counter, and asked for Scones. I thought him another American who had acquired an appetite for an ordinary breakfast food they considered exotic. I accepted payment, returned proper change, bagged the Scones, and handed them to him turning away to serve my next customer. Several days later Herb reappeared, ordered and paid for more Scones said "Thank you Miss" and left the shop without another word. Or smile. Tall. Handsome and shy. Unlike other Americans who we welcomed even though they were often loud, rude, drunk and unpleasant.

Herb was different. One day, after several more shy encounters I asked his name.

"Herbert Lerner," he said smiling.

"How do you like England?" I asked

"I like it fine. Friendly people."

"Well, we do try to make you feel welcome."

"That's true," he replied. "I like your food"

"We'll never run out of Scones."

"I hope so."

"They're not rationed, you know."

"That's smart," he replied. "I bring a thermos of hot coffee and several Scones when flying. I'm always hungry returning from a Mission."

"Our Baker will be happy to hear that.

They say -- 'Food will win the war'."

When off-duty, Herb Lerner escaped the stress of serving at an active Air Force Base by cycling country lanes bordered by old oak trees and green pastures. Ancient stone walls enclosing small farms, sod-roofed cottages, fields of new-mowed hay and grazing sheep guarded by barking dogs were a scene of breath-taking beauty in a land he swore to defend serving a cause larger than his life. He was a boy again cycling streets of his childhood now a soldier confronting the challenge of surviving a bloody war. Resting on top of a haystack, looking up at white cotton-ball clouds floating overhead, he listened to swallows singing him to sleep, his eyes closing, overcome by an intense feeling of being alive, discovering his finite place in the universe with war an insult, a degradation of life's great gifts. He felt blessed by 'Lady Luck'.

After 25 Missions, American Aircrews rotated back to the United States for rest and reassignment to other flight duties. On the wall, next to the bed in Kati's apartment, she recorded Herb's bombing Missions, happily watching the numbers grow towards the life-saving 25, sharing Herb's confidence he would survive and they would marry and live happily ever after. Yes! Yes! Herb would be alive, but what would happen to Kati when he returned to America? Could they overcome the U.S. Military's objections to war-time weddings and marry? -- 'find 'em -- feel 'em -- fuck 'em and forget them' appeared to be Official Government Policy protecting passionate G.I.'s from English girls hoping to enter the United States through pretended love. But what if that love was real? -- Was there no room for true love in US Army regulations? Each new Mission brought them closer to the day he would leave England A possibility exchanging today's happiness for a future apart. And then came the humiliation of submitting to an indifferent Army Chaplain a birth certificate, Church records and affidavits demonstrating Kati was free of all medical and legal impediments to a marriage the Chaplain recommended be postponed until Herb survived the war. After all, the Chaplain argued, "England has more than enough widowed mothers and fatherless children. We don't need another 'Lost Generation'." And then one day, the Chaplain entered her Bakery, and seeing his now grim but sympathetic face, Kati knew what he was about to say.

Kati shook her head screaming -- "No! No! No!" -- fainted and fell to the floor, sobbing like a child.

"Herb is no more," the Chaplain explained. "His remains are now buried at the American Military Cemetery at Cambridge."

A beautiful Cemetery with American flags flying over rows of white crosses set amidst green plantings and shrubs honoring the dead with solemn recognition of sacrifice in a worthy cause. At a Star of David, next to my Remembrance stone, I saw a bouquet of flowers, a token of a visitor's devotion to a memory. I wondered how after twenty years someone's eternal love still survived, prevailing over sorrow and disappointment, evoking thoughts of my mortality. I complimented a Grounds-keeper saying Americans appreciate the care and respect shown their beloved dead, pointing at Herb Learner's decorated grave.

"Oh no," he said. "I didn't do those flowers. About this time, every year, a woman comes and plants them."

"Do you know who she was? Her name," I asked. "Sometimes she comes with her son." he replied, shaking his head. "There's a Visitor's Register at the Gate House," he explained. "She always signs-in, sometimes writes her name."

440 miles in from the Libyan coast, in the wastelands of the cruel Sahara desert, the remains of my James Madison High School classmate, Bob Nassau, was discovered in 1950 half buried in a sea of Sand Dunes. In 1944, returning from bombing Naples, disoriented by a violent Sandstorm, Bob Nassau flew inland for two hours searching for his Base. With fuel tanks almost dry, and

with failing engines, he successfully landed his bomber on the back slope of a sand Dune. Uninjured, and with only nine canteens of water, Bob Nassau and his nine man crew attempted to walk to safety hoping to find Bedouin Wells that would save their lives. Travelling at night, resting during the day in shade created by an awning of parachute panels, they soon dehydrated, becoming disoriented as their body organs ceased functioning. After walking 85 miles in eight days, they collapsed and died and were covered by desert sands. A Bronze Memorial at a Libyan Military Cemetery records their names and tragic fate.

President of our High School Chess Club, Bob Nassau had remarkable intelligence and ability to evaluate two or three future moves anticipating his opponent's strategy. He was unbeatable -- humble winning, and gracious to losers. Medium height, with dark hair and eyes that made immediate contact when he spoke, he shunned Athletics with afternoon's studying and reading in the school library his favorite pastime. When he won a Four Year Scholarship to Harvard we were not surprised.

Rated a 'Superior Pilot' Bob Nassau maintained his assigned position in Formations with uncanny skill, becoming his Squadron's 'Lead Plane' guiding them to Targets dropping concentrated bomb patterns.

He was also 'Captain Luck' with aircrews eager to fly with him, confident of safely acquiring the life-saving total of 25 Missions. Also envied at 'Mail Calls', no one in the Squadron had more female 'Pen Pals' sending him mail and gifts enhancing his reputation as a Stud. His incoming Mail astounded Mail Clerks who, when holding up his letters, enthusiastically shouted "Bob Nassau" as if keeping score on his conquests.

Stranded in the desert, Bob Nassau faced the most extreme test of his leadership guiding nine men to safety. He recognized the cause of this disaster flying a Radio Direction Finder Bearing taking him past his base instead of on a course to where he could land. Human error! A real Fuck-up! by his exhausted Navigator confused after eight hours returning from their target. A fact he did not reveal to his crew.

"There will be no stragglers," he ordered. "We will stay together leaving no man behind. The strong will assist the weak. And at night, we will rest as much as possible. If we don't give up we will make it. Other crews have walked out of here."

Bob Nassau knew they landed South of their Base. The Big Dipper Constellation rotating around the North Star like the hands of a Grandfather Clock, would guide them to safety. As long as Orion rose in the East and set in the West they were not lost! Not if they continued walking North reviving in the cool night air. During the day thirst tormented them. Some, after their canteens emptied, drank their Urine and became ill. Several men hallucinated, describing an Oasis of lakes and swaying Palm trees, Mirages raising their hopes. Some, weakened and despairing, lay down in the sand and died leaving a trail of bodies partially covered by sand marking their tragic journey. And when they found a Bedouin Well it was a wet muddy twenty foot deep hole dug in the sand, and they had no rope to lower a man down to dig to reach water.

On the third day, they saw on the distant horizon, a Camel Caravan moving across the crest of a Sand Dune. Shouting and waving their arms they fired Rockets into the air hopefully watching them bursting in a multi-color display signaling their hope of rescue. The Caravan moved on, slowly disappeared, and some men, overcome by disappointment, wept.

On the eight day, delirious Bob Nassau, each step on the shifting sand an agony, began hallucinating, his tormented mind recalling triumphant Chess Matches when as Master of the board, he overwhelmed opponents with moves spectators applauded. Bob Nassau walked on, stumbling, dragging his feet as he re-played winning games. But No! No! No! Something had gone wrong this day as he re-played another game walking on and on and on -- gasping for breath -- his vision clouding -- his heart slowly beating as he heard the Umpire of Life and Death cry -- "Checkmate!"

On December 17, 1944 Sol Tyson's war ended. He felt relief and pride at how his Platoon stopped for one day an advancing SS Panzer column on a narrow road at an intersection near Malmedy Belgium. The Americans raised their arms, surrendered their weapons, and were held captive with another group of POW's, 120 G.I.'s unaware the Germans were obeying orders to take no Prisoners, show no pity, give no quarter. When the machine guns began firing, the Prisoners panicked, turned and ran into the forest, some falling to the ground pretending to be dead, while a few survived hidden in the homes of patriotic Belgium civilians. SS Officers pressed their Lugers to the necks of the wounded murdering them to insure there would be no witnesses to a War Crime. Fleeing through the Ardennes Forest 43 survivors made it thru the American lines to troops now blocking the German advance. Today, at the Malmedy War Memorial in Baugnez, Belgium, a wall of black stones honors the American dead including my friend and James Madison High School classmate Sol Tyson.

Sol Tyson was not born to be a soldier to grow up to kill some other mother's son. Quiet, enjoying reading and listening to music, he thought he might someday study at a Yeshiva after graduation. At 18 he enlisted in the army wearing 'dog tags' with the letter H identifying his religion. He ignored anti-Semitic comments, the careless speech of ignorant Draftees speaking of 'Kikes, Yids, Sheenies,' and 'Jew Boys', as a normal part of their vocabulary. Sol was of medium height, dark hair, well built, with a face revealing his ethnicity. He ignored insulting comments confident he could respond appropriately when necessary.

'Sunny Smith's Athletic Club', on Kings Highway and 17th street, Brooklyn, taught The 'Manly Art of self Defense' to Boys inspired by the historic careers of Boxing Champions Barney Ross, Benny

Leonard, Max Baer, Ruby Goldstein and Slapsie Maxi Rosenblum. When Professional Boxing became a national passion, with Championship Fights international events, Sol Tyson, although never a Contender, certainly knew how to defend himself.

Harassed by sadistic Sergeant Blinki Ralston, ordered to do extra push-ups, run more circuits of the Parade grounds, stand more hours of Guard Duty, work the Garbage Detail more often, Sol Tyson waited patiently for an opportunity to retaliate against a Bully whose eyes never ceased blinking. Every Thursday after the evening meal, a 'Happy Hour' entertainment included two rounds Boxing with Sergeant Ralston. Standing in the ring, welcoming challengers, the Sergeant laughed and joked promising to make "Grown-up Men out of boys. And if you are still standing after two rounds, you get a week-end Pass to leave Camp for forty-eight hours."

To everyone's surprise, Sol Tyson entered the ring to fight the Sergeant who was a head taller, heavier, with long arms protecting his face and body. The Sergeant was a slugger, a street fighter, not a skilled boxer. In the first round, Sol Tyson danced in and out and around his opponent, pounding his face and ribs, staggering the Sergeant now helpless against Sol's relentless attack. In the second round, merciless, Sol pounded the Sergeant attempting to shield his face with his gloves when Sol knocked him out with a savage blow to his jaw. The Sergeant fell to the floor, unconscious, his face swollen and bleeding. The audience cheered, shouted, and applauded, pounding the floor with their feet. 'Jew Boy' Sol Tyson was now their Champion.

After his defeat, Sergeant Ralston again failed to break Sol Tyson's spirit with humiliating assignments. Undaunted, happy, with Basic Training, finished, receiving orders to go overseas, Sol Tyson welcomed the opportunity to go and fight a real war.

When Herb Lerner's personal effects, sent by the U.S. Army's Grave Registration Unit arrived at her home, Rose Lerner stored them in the Attic where they remained unexamined for five years. Then one day, opening the trunk identified by Herb's name, rank and number, she found uniforms, shoes, hats, gloves, sun glasses, books, magazines, a Daily Diary and a Logbook recording Bombing Missions. Also, tied with a ribbon, a bundle of Letters. Love letters written by Kati Pollard with a photograph signed "love forever" arousing silent tears. When her eyes cleared, Rose Lerner sat quietly in the light of the Attic's window and learned about her son's war-time years. Tragic years mourning the loss of friends and expressing the joy of returning from bombing Missions alive. Rose Lerner also discovered their tender love in Kati's letters. Dozens of letters speaking of the dreams and hopes they shared in an intimate relationship of passionate love promising to bear a child. Rose Lerner's grandchild.

In 1948, The Gold Star Mothers of America organized compassionate Charter Flights to American Military Cemeteries in England, France and Belgium. Declining their offers for two years, still mourning her loss, but encouraged by the promise revealed in Kati's letters, Rose Lerner flew to England to visit Herb's grave and hopefully find Kati Pollard and her grandchild. After saying Kaddish at her son's grave, and placing a memorial stone beneath the Star of David, Rose Lerner walked to the gate house to read the Visitor's Register recording names and comments from visiting parents and children of the dead. Thousands of names and comments -- "Rest In Peace" -- "You are not forgotten" -- "A Noble Youth. Gentle, kind, beloved by all" -- were heart-breaking tributes the living paid to the dead.

The 1944 Register contained Kati Pollard's name, comments and address. A small village adjacent to a US Air Force Base with a Main street of small Shops, a traditional Anglican Church, a Pub, and rows of window flower pots in full mid-summer bloom. Rose Lerner strolled the quiet un-crowded street enjoying the fragrance and beauty of a village unchanged for centuries. 'There will always be an England' came to mind, and Yes! -- she recalled -- 'England will be free' despite national Bankruptcy, Post War Austerity, hunger, and the loss of life sacrificed to defeat Hitler.

At the Bake Shop, the young girl at the Counter nodded and politely replied -- "Yes I do know there was someone by that name working here years ago. During the war I believe. But she's been long gone ever since her family passed away."

"Do you know of anyone who would help me find her, " Rose Lerner asked.

"Well, she didn't have many friends, kept to herself, quiet like, you know."

"Yes. I imagine she was like that."

"Well you might ask our Vicar. He's been here since before the War."

The Vicar nodded, his almost sightless eyes studying Rose Lerner, his collar and grey hair confirming his vocation. He listened to Rose Lerner's reason for her visit, shaking his head, sighing, saying: "Those were heart-breaking years, you might say, terrible years, "he added, rising from his chair, going to the window where he opened the Blinds. He turned and faced his American visitor. "Truly a Time that tried Men's souls -- and also many young women" he continued as in the street outside his Study an auto horn sounded intruding on the peace and quiet of the room.

"Sorrow, heartbreak, tragedy were an inescapable part of their lives," the Vicar said -- "and Kati Pollard, and many other young girls got into trouble with all those handsome young American boys." The Vicar paused, choosing his words carefully as he explained -- "I'm afraid the Village was not very forgiving -- not charitable -- no matter what I preached. -- 'Judge Not Lest Ye be judged' -- were just words. And when she began to show her condition, she lost her job at the Bakery -- and with her parents gone -- she had no family to keep her here and help her bear her shame. She moved to London I believe."

With Post- War social Programs of the British Labor Party transforming class divisions, The National Health Service Register, for the first time in the United Kingdom provided a complete Census of the nation listing names and addresses of all citizens. Kati Pollard lived at 142 North End House, Fitz James avenue, London W14OKZ and Rose Lerner went there wondering what to do. She couldn't ring the doorbell and introduce herself. The shock of meeting Herb's mother was no way to begin a relationship. She must allow time for Kati to not see her as a threat to the life she now lived in London.

For several days Rose Lerner sat for hours on a bench at a nearby Park where children played and fed Ducks swimming on a small Pond. When Kati Pollard appeared with her son, Rose Lerner recognized Kati from photographs. She was pregnant, married, and happy. Did Rose Lerner have a right to intrude into Kati's life? Was her dream of knowing her Grandchild selfish and destructive? Watching a five year old boy at play confirmed her belief he was Herb's son recalling memories of how he walked and ran and turned his head to look back at his mother for approval. And now he had another Father. Other Grandparents. What was she doing sitting here day after day hoping to see the boy she had no right to claim as her own flesh and blood? One morning Kati Pollard appeared and sat beside her on the bench. "I think I know who you are," she said. "I'm sure Herb had your photograph with him when he died."

For the remaining weeks of her visit, Rose Lerner lived with Kati and her husband William Howard, a school teacher who adopted Herb's son and gave him his name. The Howard's were a happy family and Herb's new Father would no doubt raise him to be a fine young English gentleman. Someone Rose Lerner could be proud of and love though separated by an ocean. Kati told of Herb's high spirits, jokes, laughter and effort to enjoy life. They were very happy, Herb never declining an opportunity to sing in his lovely voice. A beautiful voice welcomed at her village Pub singing Ballads, Arias and Folk songs greeted with applause and Pints of Beer. Yes! Kati exclaimed, "It was good to be alive! And so good to remember."

Rose Lerner could not recall Herb singing. But how could she have not discovered his undaunted spirit expressed in song? Had her son found happiness, and personal fulfillment only in love and war?

Blown across the Libyan desert's moving sands, wind-driven Dunes flow over subterranean reservoirs of Oil waiting to be located, pumped out and add to the wealth of foreign corporations. British Petroleum Oil exploration crews regularly dig Test Holes and lower and explode explosives searching for returning echoes revealing underground lakes of 'Black Gold' worth one hundred dollars a barrel. Hard, lonely work under a cruel Sun raising temperatures to 115 degrees. Without water, death by dehydration is a constant threat and finding "Dry Holes" a regular disappointment.

A distant, dazzling bright reflection of sunlight, first thought a Mirage, led the Oil Explorers to the wreckage of a B-24 Bomber, with shattered wings, bent propellers and a fuselage torn apart by the destructive power of a crash landing. Searching the interior of the plane they found hats, gloves, Diaries and Parachutes of nine men who evidently survived the disaster.

The BPO Oil Explorers also discovered what would soon become known as the 'Trail of hope and Tears' marked by evidence of the survivors desperate journey with canteens, sun shelters made of parachute panels, discarded flying boots, and decaying corpses recording their heroic eighty five mile, eight day struggle to survive.

Bob Nassau's Daily Diary described their ordeal with heart-breaking calm. A few short sentences a day. Confident. Factual. Nothing but the truth. "Lady Luck." He wrote on DAY ONE -- "is a fickle Bitch, one fuck-up after another. Couldn't join the rest of the formation. Cloud cover concealed the target. Shut down a hot engine. Feathered the prop. Dumped bombs into the sea. Radio N.G. Only Nine canteens for nine good men. Surprising how danger makes you feel. Courageous? Indomitable? So what else is new, Bobby-boy? Isn't Flying on a wing and a prayer a piece of cake? What really breaks our Balls is hiking in God-damn fur-lined flying boots. Sinking into soft sand grabs your feet, each step an exhausting ordeal. Like walking in heavy mud. Bare feet brings blisters. A hell of a way to die! Blisters! Every night we hike North to the coastline we flew over. Always North! Just follow the drinking Gourd! Dear old Polaris in the center of a rotating Big Dipper counting the hours we walked every night. Yes! We're gonna make it! No doubt about it!

DAY TWO: Or I should say NIGHT TWO? Found a Bedouin Well. A dry hole twenty feet deep. No rope. Can't descend and dig in the mud for water. No way! Walking in the Moonlight casts our shadows on the sand. We must stay together. Easy to lose sight of the man ahead and wander off the trail. So far so good. Tail Gunner Bud Johnson our only straggler. We stop every hour to wait for him. Something unreal about walking at night -- like we're Ghosts before we die. Like we are here -- but not really here. Like we are in touch with something way down deep in our gut where we really live.

DAY THREE: The Fires of Hell. Dig Fox Holes deep in the sand, sheltered by Parachute panels. We don't move. Don't talk. Try to sleep. Conserve energy praying for the cool of the night to come before we fried. Sun burned. Dehydrated. Blistered faces. Half our water gone. SNAFU! Situation normal -- all fucked up!

DAY FOUR: Water gone. Leave behind empty Canteens marking our trail. Some talk about drinking their urine if only they could Pee. Bud Johnson gone. We stopped and waited an hour for him but he couldn't keep up with us. No one had the strength to go back and search for him.

DAY FIVE: Followed a Camel Caravan track to a Bedouin well. A day and a night drinking, sleeping, and peeing. Cursed our stupidity discarding Canteens. Must go on without carrying water hoping to find another well.

DAY SIX: Hallucinations! Mirages. Shimmering lakes and Oases. Palm trees calling to us as one by one, we lay down in the sand and die. Four more gone. Halsey. Conwell. Rosenberg. Polanski. Good men! Rest in Peace!

DAY SEVEN: Sun blind. Am I staggering through the night always North? Can't see the Stars. Night sky blurred. Can't find Howard and Ford. Are they behind me? Or ahead? Am I the last man standing? God only knows.

DAY EIGHT: Sunset. A few more words before I go. Anyone finding these pages should not break faith with we who die -- for these deaths -- our sacrifices -- give meaning to our lives -- we did not die in vain!

Kampfgruppe Roth, commanded by SS-Sturmbannführer Joachim Roth, driving through 12 Belgium towns and villages murdered 362 POW's and 111 Civilians following orders from General Seth Dietrich commanding the 6th SS Panzer Army. Employing tactics ravaging Russia, terrorizing and slaughtering civilians, burning homes and villages was an illegal German strategy evoking the fear, panic and defeatism that defeated the larger better armed French Armies in May, 1940. The German High Command believed making war on civilians as well as soldiers made 'Deutschland Uber Alles' inevitable. When Sol Tyson lay dying at a crossroad near Malmedy Belgium, SS Obersturmführer Joachim Roth pressed his Lugar to the back of Sol's head and without further thought murdered him. Repeating atrocities inflicted in Russia evoked fear and defeatism in Belgium civilians. In Russia, Joachim Roth destroyed entire villages leaving thousands homeless and starving. In Krasnaya Polyana, a Russian village, no one was alive when Roth transferred to the Western Front to repeat his horrors at the Battle of the Bulge.

At the 1946 Dachau War Crimes Trials Joachim Roth was convicted and sentenced to death. With the New Germany about to enter NATO and participate in the Cold War, and responding to German feelings that revenge and not Justice had been done, Joachim Roth's sentence was commuted to life in Prison. After 11 years he was freed and then worked as a Sales Manager for Porsche and Volkswagen.

Retiring in 1974, recalling his happy year in Paris, Joachim Roth moved to Traves, a small French country village where he hoped to raise and support his family working as a Translator. For two years he lived the good life, built a home in the woods outside the village, and enjoyed the privacy he sought by fleeing the guilt, shame and political turmoil of post-war Germany.

Café Liberty was the site of monthly meetings of the 'Association of Resistance Fighters' who drank liters of Vin Rouge, sang Patriotic songs, and dined voraciously on Cassolette and Brook Trout Amandine. Devoted Patriots, their idea of Justice included shaving heads of French women who slept with German soldiers during the Occupation, shaming them paraded naked through the village for the sadistic pleasure of patriotic French citizens.

The Villagers were aware of their secluded German neighbor, accepting his presence until a former Resistance returned from Germany carrying a Magazine with Joachim Roth's picture on the cover. A heroic photo in full uniform displaying the Medals, arrogance, pride and ruthlessness of a soldier in Germany's criminal military organization the SS -- Hitler's Pride and Glory!

A vandalized Mail Box was the first demonstration of the Villager's hostility to Joachim Roth. Then, painted on the highway leading to his home, a double Lightening SS symbol bearing Roth's name revealed his unwelcome presence.

In 1976, motivated by the anger, shame, fears and privations of the German occupation, a Fire Bomb destroyed Joachim Roth's home. His badly charred body was returned to Germany for burial in the Roth family plot with full military honors.

Joachim Roth's mother gave birth to her only son on November 8, 1923, without the comforting presence of his father, Hans Roth who was otherwise engaged. As one of 2,000 National Socialists he accompanied Hitler, Goering, Rohm, Rudolf Hess and General Erich Von Ludendorff in marching to Munich's Beer Hall in a failed attempt to overthrow the Criminal government that "stabbed the German Army in the back" by signing the humiliating Versailles Treaty. Opposed by loyal Bavarian State Police firing live ammunition, Hitler threw himself on the ground, wounded Hermann Goering turned and fled, while proud, heroic General Von Ludendorff marched on unhurt.

Inspired by Benito Mussolini's 1922 demonstration of political power with his 'March on Rome', Adolf Hitler's Beer Hall Putsch misjudged his popularity ignoring Germany's Conservative Industrialists and aristocratic Generals who regarded Hitler and the Nazi party with contempt.

Following the humiliating 1918 Armistice, Hans Roth was one of thousands of discharged soldiers bitter and angry at the 'Jew government' of democrats and socialists who betrayed the Army making their sacrifice defending Germany futile. Unemployed, Hans Roth joined the Freikorps, a civilian Militia of Brown Shirted Storm Troopers who paraded singing patriotic songs, shouting "Juden Raus" as they disrupted socialist political rallies, attacking Communists and Jews, proclaiming National Socialists the 'Wave of The Future' making 'Germany great again.'

Joachim Roth was indeed his Father's son joining the Hitler Youth organization at the age of ten, proudly wearing a uniform, parading and singing at every commemoration for fallen Nazi heroes. At summer camps he hiked and swam and learned combat Infantry tactics. Gathered around Campfires, Joachim Roth listened to 'Blood and Soil' lectures, a doctrine of 'Will and Power' teaching him to avoid 'racial defilement' and defend the purity of the Aryan race. He learned the joys of Comradeship becoming one of 8 million Hitler Youth enlisting in the notorious Adolf Hitler SS Panzer Division. The 'New Barbarians' devastating Europe and Russia.

Visiting a 'League of German Women' summer camp, Joachim Roth lost his virginity in the arms of a patriotic 'Deutscher Madel' fulfilling her obligation to provide Hitler with more soldiers pledged to die so that Germany might live.

A ninety day Blitzkrieg conquering France, Belgium and Holland confirmed all Joachim Roth had been taught about Aryan racial superiority. Seeing French soldiers abandon their weapons, raising their arms, shamelessly surrendering, cheering as they became Prisoners, was astonishing. Their War was over. Joachim Roth's war had just begun.

The June 1941 Blitzkrieg invasion of Russia was stalled by the vastness of the Steppes unpaved roads with rainstorms making them Bogs. Snow and bitter cold of an early winter prevented repeating the 1940 conquest of Western Europe. Wearing summer uniforms, Hitler Youth, now veteran soldiers, found their destiny freezing and dying in the ruins of Stalingrad where 90,000 were abandoned by Hitler who ordered them to die writing another glorious page in German History.

"I always obeyed orders," Joachim Roth wrote in his War Diary. "I violated International Law executing Jewish Commissars and subhuman Russians fighting a war of competing ideologies liquidating without mercy all opposed to National Socialism. Hitler absolved soldiers violating the 'Rules of War' making our army and SS SonderKommandos, an Army of murderers. Burning homes, destroying villages, executing civilians, our Panzer Armies commanded by General Von Manstein killed half a million homeless, starving Peasants. We came, and for more than a year, we conquered creating a wasteland ravaged by Famine.

When you kill an enemy, something within you dies in exchange for the highs of combat and the exhilaration of victory. After several months attacking, advancing, killing and destroying, an overwhelming sense of dread and gloom saddened my days and sleepless nights. I felt I was suffocating. Drowning. Exhausted. I became confused, disconnected, and feared losing my mind. I could not remember yesterday's events. Anguished. Tormented. I wondered -- Am I going mad? -- Relieved of my Command, and after months recuperating in a Hospital, I was ordered to France to fight Americans and fulfill my destiny as a German soldier."

At least 'Once in Paris' was a High Command order insuring every German soldier would enjoy the historic achievements of Western culture. The avenues, statues, Cathedrals, Museums, theaters, restaurants, and Night Clubs described in a Guidebook included the Louvre, Sacre Coeur, Montmartre, the Moulin Rouge, Place de la Concorde, and the Trocadero where soldiers had their first view of the great triumphs of the human spirit. Officers lived at the Ritz and dined at Maxims and La Coupole. Foot soldiers were serviced at Brothels, Rest and Recreation facilities offering intercourse and intoxication to an occupying army wandering Paris like hungry tourists. French Celebrities and Movie Stars Maurice Chevalier, Edith Piaf, Collette, Daniel Darrieux and Arletty entertained German's with France's greatest actress saying -- "My heart belongs to France -- but my ass is International."

But what of the Parisians who regarded German correct behavior with disdain? Enduring 9 PM to 5 AM Curfews, pervasive hunger and cold and the humiliation of seeing a Swastika flying over the Arc de Triumph, Paris tolerated the intolerable until the murder of a German officer ended a year of peaceful and profitable co-existence. Retaliating, the SS executed 981 hostages. The French Gendarmes, imposing Nazi racial laws, cooperating with Germany's 'deliver on demand' order, rounded up 13,152 Jews, ultimately transporting 78,000 to Auschwitz.

The Bois de Bulounge was Joachim Roth's favorite Parisian attraction where he would stroll for hours amidst trees and flowers reminding him of the forests he played in during his childhood. Homesick, lonely, Roth tried to understand feelings aroused by seeing in Paris possibilities he never imagined or been exposed to. Nazi 'Will and Power' indoctrinated with torch lit parades, marching and singing with raised arms saluting their exalted Leader, with Propaganda films presenting beliefs he now questioned, he wondered, was he his father's son repeating his fanatical devotion to Germany's triumphant future? Or was he someone with other thoughts, feelings and destiny? With the fall of France, with only England defying Germany, and Europe ruled by Hitler, the war would soon end and he would return to a nation different from the culture he enjoyed in Paris. 'Paris always conquers the Conquers' was an historic truth Joachim Roth was now experiencing.

Resting on a park bench, watching strollers and cyclists in summer clothing passing by with young families opening picnic baskets under the trees, with children shouting and running playing games, Joachim Roth recognized he had become a man struggling to understand his obedience to criminal orders.

In occupied Paris where bicycles and tricycle Cabs replaced Taxis for public transportation, Simone Le Moine's favorite cycling path was in the Bois de Boulange thru an avenue of old trees and flowering shrubs perfuming the air with nature's intoxicating beauty. Exhilarated by exercise, her lungs and heart filling with health and strength, Simone Le Moine, a young, beautiful Parisian welcomed each new day. With the Armistice signed and France returning to Peace and Prosperity guided by Marshal Petain restoring France's ancient glory, Simone imagined a future free of hunger and fear.

A small stone in the cycling path deflected her front wheel, and before Simone could regain her balance, she tumbled over the handle bars falling to the ground. Dazed, bruised, almost unconscious but not seriously injured, Simone lay inert a moment before attempting to rise. Then, raised to her feet, and led to a park bench, she opened her eyes and saw the compassionate smile of a handsome German soldier, Joachim Roth. His eyes were kind, comforting, Simone felt no fear.

"You had quite a fall, mademoiselle."

"Thank you for your help," Simone replied in German.

"How come you speak my language?"

"I'm from Alsace Lorraine."

"The Provinces Germany once occupied?"

"Yes," Simone answered, nodding.

"Well, all Occupations end, " Roth said, as if stating a great truth. "I hope so," Simone replied. "The sooner the better."

"Yes. I agree." Roth said, smiling. Then, after a brief pause he said: "I've seen you here before."

"My favorite ride thru these beautiful woods."

"Reminds me of the forests near my village. I come here to recall my childhood."

"I have seen you."

"My home away from home," Roth laughed. "I flee from the crowd to dwell with peace and truthfulness."

"Yes. I understand. Sometimes Paris can be too much."

"May I ask -- Why did you never stop and say hello?"

"You are my enemy."

"Really? Tell me, do I look like an enemy?"

"No."

"No matter how correct Germans behave, we are not always welcomed."

"It's the War."

'Yes, the war. But now we have peace. Only poor foolish

England continues fighting."

Simone rose from the bench, and before mounting her bicycle and riding away, turned and said -- "Thank you again. You are very kind."

And it's true, Simone thought as she continued her ride thinking Germans are human beings doing their duty, wearing different uniforms, saluting different Leaders. What is a good patriotic French girl to do? Salute our flag, pledge allegiance to Petain and hate? How should we behave waiting for our young men, husbands and lovers to return from POW Camps and forced labor in Germany? Could be years before we see them again and life becomes normal. Yes -- how should we behave with all those lonely hungry German soldiers wandering Paris like homesick cattle? Ignore them? Pity them? And what should I do tomorrow? Where do I ride? There are other bicycle paths in these woods. I am not compelled to return here again. Yes. In my heart I will always be a French Patriot singing La Marseilles celebrating the return of our Provinces. And certainly I am not a perfect Patriot. I am just who I am struggling for happiness with many affairs. Broken many hearts including my own. But never cruel. Always loving. Always loving. And who knows what tomorrow will bring? Peace? More War? More hate? The Resistantes would have falling in love with a German a reason for shame! Treason! Disloyalty! Have they never felt the intense feeling, the undeniable power that stops your heart and takes your breath away? Am I not entitled to some happiness, some escape from the death, destruction, hunger and fear that war brings to victims of every nationality? German or French? What is the difference? We all suffer.

And certainly this young German is handsome. Has a kind face. Beautiful blue eyes that looked right into my soul.

TWO

Sol Tyson, born Solomon Tissenbaum on March 12th 1925, legally changed his name becoming a naturalized U.S. citizen at the Federal Courthouse in New York. Fleeing Germany, his family's first American home was a two room cold-water flat on Delancy street in Manhattan's lower East side Ghetto. Aaron, his father, a skilled garment cutter, worked 12 hours a day in a Manhattan sweat shop supporting Sol and his mother Sarah. After two years living with a courtyard Privy as their toilet, they moved to Ocean avenue Brooklyn and a better life in an apartment with hot water, bathtub, toilet and shower. The American Dream come true.

At PS-197, Sol struggled to learn English and pass exams enabling him to enter High School. As a Special student he was tutored by compassionate teachers who taught Sol to read, write, do arithmetic and learn about the American government in Civics classes. At James Madison High School by diligent academic effort Sol earned grades in the New York State Regents exams qualifying him to enter Brooklyn College. Reacting to Pearl Harbor, Sol did not ask for a Student Draft deferment patriotically enlisting in the US Army.

Dear Poppa -- Sol wrote home -- I am on a Troopship steaming to France. 5,000 G.I.'s going to war -- many are immigrant sons -- their fathers come from Ekatrinislav, Kiev, Odessa, Warsaw, Minsk, Vilna to escape Pogroms, work hard and earn their share of the Golden Medina -- the American dream. Also onboard are the Fighting Irish from Manhattan and Italians from Brooklyn singing

-- 'When Tony goes over the Top -- keep your eye on the fighting Wop.'

We wait our turn for sleeping eight hours in Bunk beds that are always warm, and every twelve hours eat food that is often cold. The Latrines smell worse than Delancey street outhouses, and when the ocean is rough the ship's rails are crowded with the seasick heaving their meals overboard. No longer bullied and scorned I'm a soldier of the United States Army, an American. Thank you for having the courage to abandon everything in the old country to bring me where I have the opportunity to live as a free man among men. No small achievement. A great gift -- Freedom! So don't worry -- I have no intentions of dying for my country. I want to live, know failure or success. -- I'll be the difference -- I guess.

Please kiss Momma for me -- Love Sol.

"Greenhorns -- Peanuts! Popcorns! Five cents a box!" shouted bullies reminding Immigrants they were unwelcome. Insults and hatred Sol recalled as he lay dying, and before Joachim Roth put a bullet in his brain Sol felt a dark curtain descending over the final moments of his life, and there would be no encore, no applause welcoming Sol to whatever exists on the other side called death. I'm too young to die, Sol protested. Too young. Too young. Too young. Dying, Sol Tyson saw his father returning home every evening, exhausted, worn out from the drudgery of his life. And his mother cooking and cleaning and sewing and adoring her only child. Could they get along without him, he wondered? What else did they have to make their lives worth living? -- Man does not live by bread alone, and give us this day our daily bread he remembered as he said good bye to the world. Good bye -- Good bye world -- it's been good to know you -- if only for eighteen years. -- I'm going -- going -- gone -- but there's no rush! No rush! I know how to wait. There's so much more to think about like what's it like to fall in love, marry, and have a child.

I'll never know -- never -- never know -- never know -- never!

THREE

"The Clown Prince" of James Madison High School. Herb Lerner was one of many renowned Alumni including an Olympic Athlete, a Supreme Court Justice, a Senator, a Movie Star, a Comedian and a notorious Attorney who defended criminals, rapists, murderers, and Mafia Godfathers.

Herb Lerner discovered the remarkable healing power of laughter during The Great Depression of the 1930's when Walt Disney's animated cartoon "Who's Afraid of The Big Bad Wolf" changed our Nation's mood from fear to hope. "Now's the Time to Fall in Love" made "The Hit Parade" of best-selling records, and Kate Smith singing -- "God Bless America" amplified President Roosevelt's advice -- "We have nothing to fear -- but Fear itself."

Comedy, laughter, jokes, good or bad, were as necessary as the air Herb breathed and He knew what he wanted to do in the future years of his life. Herb Lerner had a joke for every occasion. Bar Mitzvahs. Weddings. Funerals, Graduations -- nothing was sacred. Nothing beyond the touch of Herb Lerner's wit. His comic gift.

A gift born of tragedy. At the age of twelve, his beloved father Aaron died taking away Herb Learner's feeling of well-being and high hopes. He felt life will never be the same without an angry, loving, hard-working father to scold and slap and teach him the ways of the Torah. Herb Lerner felt he was a spiritual Orphan, someone forever bereft, forever mourning irreplaceable loss. Sleepless nights, dark thoughts and despair were concealed behind his comic routines. We laughed, applauded and welcomed his jokes, asking for more, unaware of his pain, unaware of Herb's conversations with his father who reappeared and could not be denied at critical moments of his life. Herb's jokes were often savage, insulting friendly audiences hungry for more laughter, more satire, more denial of the pity and heartbreak of War. Herb Lerner laughed and sang and entertained in the skies over Germany, and, in his bomber, on final approach to the runway that became his funeral Pyre, I wondered what were Herb Lerner's closing lines? His final bow to a Fate that interred his burned and charred remains in a Military Cemetery in Cambridge England?

During the 1930's Bob Nassau learned of the Oxford University debate saying "No!" to the proposition -- "One must fight for King and Country!". A denial of Patriotism that shocked Great Britain calling students "Despicable cowards. Unworthy of our great heritage." The Philosopher William James, proposing a "Moral equivalent to War" inspired Bob Nassau to support Charles Lindberg spokesman for the "America First" Committee's attempt "To Keep America out of war". Anne Morrow Lindberg's best-selling "Wave of The Future" advocated acceptance of Hitler's Germany as preferable to War. A Peace Rally in Berkeley California, in April 1940, confirmed Bob Nassau's conviction he must become a Conscientious Objector who would morally resist the Draft.

Fascism's victory in Spain, and Germany's conquest of Europe with the shameful surrender of Paris convinced Bob Nassau there are times when war is the only acceptable choice. Writing an Editorial in the Harvard Crimson explaining his changed beliefs, he enlisted in the Air Force urging other students to meet the challenge of another war to save Peace and Democracy.

Helen Schary, an East 28th street neighbor with long golden hair and inviting eyes was Bob Nassau's first true love. They were Best Friends who grew up together playing childhood games, roller skating, walking pet dogs, celebrating birthdays and going to movies where they often held hands, and occasionally kissed innocent kisses. Adoring parents approved and thought they were made for each other and would someday marry. A blessed event uniting two fine families. Their Grammar and High School years were a joyous prelude to a future when they would marry and raise a family repeating the inevitable life cycle of faithful love and devotion.

Soon after Helen's fourteenth Birthday, a joyous event, Helen Schary began having difficulty remembering and speaking as if connections between her brain and body had been severed. Despite sleeping long hours and taking mid-day naps, Helen's energy faded. Playing games, walking to school, became difficult and then impossible. Confined to bed, Helen never again left her room free of the consequences of Multiple Sclerosis. An insidious disease where a patient's contact with others gradually disappeared.

For more than a year, Bob Nassau sat at Helen's Schary's bedside every afternoon watching the 'love of his life' slowly fade away. Unable to speak with Helen, Bob Nassau fought back tears, holding her hand, smiling, whispering words of undying love that were unanswered. Bob Nassau witnessed and shared her torment, grieving, agonizing, acquiring deep painful wounds that would be with him forever.

Without borders, the chemistry of love is truly international with allegiance only to the human heart. Joachim Roth and Simone Le Moine never enjoyed the pleasures of Lovers strolling the Champs Elysee. Nor could they sit for hours at sidewalk Cafes drinking Aperitifs watching Parisian life pass by. Roth's uniform provoked disapproving looks arousing a desire for privacy in the back rooms of small Cafes where maître d's and waiters reluctantly served and rarely welcomed them. Only in Simone's apartment, ignoring the Concierge's hostility could they enjoy the intimate joys of Lovers.

Simone Le Moine believed she was not a Collaborator benefiting from France's defeat. Nor was she like government officials, the Police and movie stars accommodating their lives and careers to the reality of occupied France. Was she unpatriotic? Simone wondered, was she betraying her country falling in love with Joachim Roth?

Simone and Joachim found their lovers sanctuary on the Seine floating downstream past ancient buildings and riverside parks that witnessed centuries of France's glorious history. The songbirds, old trees and blooming flowers on the river banks confirmed the survival of 'France Eternal', a people who can never be defeated. They had no doubt the German Occupation will pass and Liberty, Equality and Fraternity will again prevail allowing their great love to continue without shame.

They enjoyed an Idyllic year of love discovering each other. Becoming one in desire and understanding of love's possibilities. Experiencing new, profound feelings, Joachim Roth recognized and valued Simone's generous love. That this bliss could continue forever seemed an impossible dream. A year in a world foreign to everything Joachim Roth had been taught -- suddenly ended in June 1941 with the German Army's invasion of Russia appropriately named -- "Operation Barbarossa". The attack of the Barbarians. -- And Joachim Roth would soon be one of them.

FOUR

August 18th 1944, a General Strike in Paris led by 1,600 "Resistantes" paralyzed the city with Factory Workers, Police, Metro, Food and Bus services demonstrating against the German Occupation. With General Patton's Third Army liberating northern France, General Phillipe Le Clerc's 2nd French Armored Division drove South to Paris entering the City on August 19 parading down the Champs-Élysées welcomed by ecstatic crowds dancing and singing 'La Marseillaise'. Six days of street fighting, with Snipers firing at civilians made Parisian avenues battlefields defended by all Partisans able to carry a gun. On August 25th, General Dietrich Von Choltitz, defying Hitler's order to totally destroy Paris, surrendered the City, an event celebrated by General Charles de Gaulle marching down the Champs-Élysées declaring: "Today we salute fighting France, heroic France, true France, Eternal France liberating France by itself."

General Dietrich Von Choltitz fought in Poland, and Holland witnessing the destruction of Warsaw and Rotterdam, great cities reduced to rubble. A tragic sight to a veteran of two world wars. When appointed Military Governor of Paris, advised by Hitler to expect future orders to destroy 'The City of Light', General Choltitz wondered would he be capable of such senseless barbarism. Would he ignore direct orders to burn the Capitol of Western civilization before abandoning it? Would he refuse to answer Hitler's hysterical question: "Is Paris Burning?"

'Duty is my Honor' was the core belief of his life and career. Would he ever fail to do his duty, be insubordinate and betray a tradition followed by three generations of the Choltitz military family? He opposed SS Officers, angered by the assassination of

General Student preventing them from murdering Dutch Prisoners, an atrocity he considered a violation of the Military Code of Honor. Ambitious Generals accepting Hitler's military plans, knowing they were futile, doomed to fail, placing their careers above the best interests of the Fatherland -- he thought a betrayal of all he believed -- and by not protesting had he condoned their violations of The Rules of War commanded an army of murderers? Believing Hitler to be insane, and motivated by his love of the city, General Choltitz, obeying his conscience -- chose to be remembered as "The Savior of Paris".

Liberation initiated months of shameful 'Legal Purifications' when revenge against Collaborators murdered anyone guilty of cooperating with the German Occupation. Informers, Black Market Profiteers, Gendarmes and sadistic members of the Milice, the French SS, were assassinated in a ruthless reign of terror. 'Horizontal Collaborators' -- women sleeping with German soldiers -- were paraded through the streets of Paris naked, heads shaved, smeared with excrement by sadistic Patriots revenging years of hunger and humiliation. Prostitutes working in Paris's celebrated Brothels who thrived servicing German soldiers were pardoned for doing what was expected of them in 'The City of Light and Joy!'

Simone Le Moine, fearing the horrors of Liberation, pregnant with Joachim Roth's child, fled to St Agathe, her childhood village where she hoped to find sanctuary and escape 'Legal Purification.' To her friends and family Simone described her Lover as a French Prisoner in Germany with whom she was engaged to marry when the war ended. To maintain her deception, she wrote letters to the Army Postal Service for forwarding to a Prisoner who existed only in her imagination.

"Dear Claude," Simone wrote, "the war will soon end and with the Occupation gone you will take me in your arms and we will know the bliss that is our destiny. We will live in the New France our beloved Marshall Petain will create free of hunger, fear and despair. When you are no more a Prisoner of War, a forced Laborer working for your enemy, you will return to a better France where we will marry and raise a family to love and be proud of. I have no words to tell you how much I miss your embraces, memories that give me the strength to wait for you with the profound joy of a love where two have become one forever inseparable. Our son will inherit your courage, your strength, your devotion to all the best virtues of our beloved France. 'France Eternal' as General De Gaulle said. Free France where we will marry and live happily ever after. Hopefully there will be no more war. Peace will be our only choice after all we have experienced since 1940. Mankind will chose life over death making love not War! And our son will never be drafted to fight for God or Country or whatever Politicians declare are reasons worth dying for. Never! Never! Certainly what is growing inside me will live only with those capable of enduring love -- and refusing to hate we will watch our son become a free and honorable man. Tell me dear Claude -- tell me -- Am I dreaming an impossible dream?

Love always." Simone.

Joachim Roth's son Jacques recalls a childhood feeling alone and uncared for with days and nights governed by bells to awaken, feed or announce the time to sleep on a Pallet on a dormitory floor. Nuns with white Cowls, pale faces and soft voices floated over his crib, Ghosts who never held him in their arms in a loving embrace. Untouched, cold, alone, only when Simone visited did Jacques Le Moine experience the reassuring comfort of human warmth. A tin cup and a small bowl brought food and drink, daily prayers awakened his soul while memorizing his Catechism Jacques Le Moine fulfilled his duty to God.

Simone Le Moine fulfilled her maternal duties when she married and provided a father and home for Jacques removing him from his barren life with Nuns. Jacques remembered wearing a child's silk Nightshirt, the sights and sounds and cooking odors of his first home. He remembered crawling across a hard wooden floor, struggling to stand and be picked up and embraced in his mother's arms. He remembered his foster father singing him to sleep. He remembered looking around the room discovering the world, faces and sights so different from his years as a homeless unloved child. He remembered when he cried someone responded to his call for food or warmth or cleanliness. He remembered he had a name and his name was Jacques and when someone called out to him he smiled. He remembered his past, memories he could recall when searching for his own true and unique identity as he became a young man finding his own place in a confusing chaotic world. Memories were his most precious possession and Jacques Le Moine recognized he was more than the sum total of his memories.

Jacques excelled as a student at the village Lycee. A typical young handsome French boy who played games in the streets and on soccer fields. He cycled thru woods surrounding his village and swam in the river that flowed past his town. He flirted with girls who laughed and sang and danced and shyly gave him his first kiss. And reading of the next inevitable war he abandoned going to a University. At 18, drafted into the French Army fighting an unpopular war to regain her Indo-China Colonies, Jacques discovered he thrived as a soldier. The order and discipline fighting to bring Liberty, Equality and Fraternity to the uncivilized, seemed an honorable profession. As an officer, Jacques felt destined to risk and possibly give his life for France. The country he loved.

Ordered to burn Vietnamese villages and force homeless Farmers into fortified Strategic Hamlets where they could no longer hide and feed Viet Minh Insurgents, Jacques Le Moine accepted the logic of military barbarism. Ho Chi Minh's rebels were day-time farmers who attacked at night, killing government officials, destroying French forts, blocking highways in a war that could not be won without winning the hearts and minds of the Viet Minh enemy.

In Dien bien Phu, a North Vietnam valley, encircled by mountains, the French established what they expected would become an invincible stronghold supplied by air, dominating all of central Vietnam, insuring ultimate victory in a protracted war. A strategic blunder by over-confident Generals graduates of France's famous École de Guerre.

Strategically brilliant Vietnamese General Giap, leading his Viet Minh troops and heavy artillery on the thousand mile Hi Chi Minh Trail from Laos, encircled and trapped French Paratroopers at Dien bien phu bombarding them relentlessly from concealed positions on the surrounding mountains. After eight weeks of savage shelling by large caliber guns firing high explosives, the French, unable to air supply more food and ammunition surrendered 12,000 troops who became Viet Minh prisoners. Marching five hundred miles thru a forbidding jungle to North Vietnamese POW Camps, only 3,000 survived to be repatriated when the 1954 Geneva Peace Treaty was signed.

"A defeat of the West by the East. A triumph of the Primitive" declared a Post-War French government committee studying their humiliating surrender repeating the arrogance that produced a military disaster. That General Giap was a better General was an embarrassment too humiliating for the French to admit.

Jacques Le Moine, struggling to stay alive on a ball of rice and a canteen of water a day, did not suffer the malarial fever or cholera tormenting weaker prisoners. He walked thru the jungle one of an army of despair and starvation urged forward by the bayonets of peasants who defeated their former rulers. At night, sleeping on ground teeming with ants and jungle rats, he prayed for the strength to survive another day of torment. When Jacques Le Moine staggered and fell, Comrades raised him to his feet, supporting his emaciated body as he counted steps that became miles to an unknown destination. At noon, gathered around pots cooking their daily rice ration, Jacques Le Moine experienced the love uniting Prisoners in a bond he could not name. Jacques Le Moine also admired Sergeant Max Schultz, a French Foreign Legionnaire, one of thousands of German veterans with no profession but soldiering who left devastated Germany to help France retain her Colonies. Promised citizenship after three years, the Legionnaires were France's most experienced soldiers.

As a veteran of SS Panzer Group Roth, Max Schultz, known as Sergeant Max, had no memory for names, but never forgot the faces of soldiers he led to die in battle. Smiling or somber, sad or glad, grim or determined, there was something unmistakably French about their faces. SS 'Blood and Soil' propaganda taught him what he needed to know to recognize Aryan features in conscripts he commanded. Six years of German occupation altered the genetic inheritance of many French soldiers producing 'Blitz babies', a heritage of love affairs disrupted by defeat and retreat in 1945.

Jacques Le Moine's blond hair, fair skin, and blue eyes were clearly Aryan. More disturbing to Sergeant Max was something familiar about Jacques Le Moine. A face from a past Sergeant Max could not forget. No doubt this young French soldier had a German father.

Jacques Le Moine could not understand Sergeant Max's concern for his survival. On 'search and destroy' missions Jacques Le Moine was never the 'Point Man'. The first soldier in the Platoon to encounter enemy fire in deadly ambushes. Jacques Le Moine's unquestioned obedience to orders, his enthusiasm for doing what he had to do without hesitation reminded Sergeant Max of someone he admired. His commanding SS Officer, Obersturmbannführer -- Joachim Roth.

FIVE

Take up the White Man's Burden
the savage Wars of Peace --
Fill the mouth full of Famine
and bid the Sickness cease.

Rudyard Kipling

Royal Air Force Flight Lieutenant Herbert Howard was indeed his father's son with a bright smile, confident manner, optimism and expectation for a future promised by a happy childhood. At ten he attended a prestige Boarding School where on the Playing Fields of England and in the Chapel he learned 'Duty, honor, God and country and how Britannia Rules The Waves' because 'The Sun never sets on the British Flag.'

In 1945, with Germany and Japan defeated, with India achieving Independence, and with British Malaya threatened by Communist Insurgents, British Colonialism was challenged by Mankind's desire for Life Liberty and the Pursuit of happiness. A hope shared by all races religions and skin color. In Southeast Asia the 'White Man's Burden' became consigned to 'The dust bin of history'.

Despite Kati Howard and Rose Lerner's objections, Herbert Howard enlisted in the Royal Air Force bombing Malaysian Hamlets driving five hundred thousand Peasants into 'New Villages' enclosed by barbed wire separating them from Insurgents sheltered in the surrounding jungle. Starving Communist Rebels, murdering women and children in 'Search and Destroy' missions, defoliating their Jungle shelters with Agent Orange and Napalm fire bombs, Britain fought a ruthless Counter-Insurgency war.

Herbert Howard thought about Herb Lerner bombing Germany. What did his father feel witnessing the Fire storm destruction of Dresden where 135,000 died in two hours? What did he think at 20,000 feet flying above massive incinerations of civilians? Did liberating Europe, defeating German Barbarians justify War Crimes? Flying in tight defensive formations, surviving Flack and enemy fighters, his father certainly had no time for questions of right or wrong, no thoughts of "Te Absolvo" from the Chaplains blessing the Bomber he flew. A Holy Weapon of War.

Bombing from an altitude of 1000 feet, confident the Insurgents were defenseless from air attack, Herb Howard could see and smell the burning forests and villages, see the Peasants fleeing from their homes, see bombs striking targets in expanding blossoms of fire, blood and death. He could not distance himself from the horrors he witnessed. But this is war, he believed, not murder. That he was enabling Great Britain retain profitable Rubber Plantations was a fact he did not consider.

In the evening, drinking at the Officers Mess after another mission, he often sang -- loud and clear -- in a voice inherited from his father -- "It's a long way to Tipperary -- a long way to home -- it's a long way to Tipperary -- to the dearest girl I know".

Exhausted, with pain washed away by drink, he slept the sleep of a troubled warrior who would rise at dawn to be briefed for his next Mission and not question what he was ordered to do.

Suffering relentless stress bombing primitive jungle targets, without decisive results, Herb Howard questioned a war without victory. Can they ever defeat Peasants who will prevail no matter how high the 'Body Count' Herb Howard wondered as he dropped more bombs pursuing the 'light at the end of the Tunnel', a fool's errand prolonging a war because his government could never admit defeat, never recognize a modern Army's limitations fighting Insurgents to retain Rubber Plantations that were never bombed, but protected in a frustrating war. How many more lives will be wasted for how many more years became a question Herb Howard could not answer. He recalled Poet Wilfred Owen saying -- "My friend, you would not tell with such high zest to children ardent for some desperate glory, -- the old lie -- Dulce et decorum est Pro patria more. -- How sweet it is to die for one's country."

Herb Howard believed he had done something monstrous laying waste to entire countries, turning the evil of the enemy back upon them. Something within him had been shattered when killing more starving civilian refugees than soldiers. He felt no pride in what he had done. He felt a haunting melancholy in his heart.

Herb Howard refused to fly another Mission. He surrendered his wings to his Squadron Commander asking to be grounded -- saying -- "I've had it. I've done my bit." Diagnosed with "Chronic Battle Fatigue" Herb Howard was confined in a Psychiatric Hospital with expectations he would recover and soon return and do his duty to God and Country.

With the flood gates of his rage wide open Herb Howard never again added to the two hundred thousand casualties of Britain's anti-colonial war. Horrified by the arrogance, stupidity, and indifference of politicians serving their political ambitions, Herb Howard's anger could not be relieved by Therapists. After months of futile treatment he requested a medical discharge becoming a passionate Anti-War activist.

Herb Howard recalled Rudyard Kipling's Poem describing soldiers marching to battle in the Boer War -- "Boots -- Men go mad watching them -- Boots -- moving up and down again -- with no end in the war!" -- A truth about wars no matter how many bombs are dropped on children. No one records a 'Body Count' on children, battle-field trash too insignificant to be counted, an obscenity committed by Generals and Presidents defending their nation's security.

"What do wars do to us? -- what do we win or lose in wars?" Herb Howard asked. "Are we, like our fathers, ravaging cultures we do not understand, fighting wars because of our inability to find alternatives to death and destruction? Is Peace only a brief intermission between wars? -- Is Peace an impossible dream?"

After 12,000 French soldiers surrendered to the Viet Minh on May 7th 1954, they marched 500 miles to Prison Camps in Northern Vietnam where only 3013 survived and were repatriated by the Geneva Peace Treaty. In a notorious Death March, Jacques Le Moine and Sergeant Max, prodded by bayonets, endured hunger, exhausting heat and tropical jungle fevers draining all but their determination to survive. At night, sleeping in self-protective groups they fought off Viet Minh guards raping or killing stragglers too weak to resist. Desperate Prisoners, breaking away from the column, attempting to escape to Laos, died in a jungle of poisonous snakes and man-eating Tigers.

Who was Sergeant Max? Jacques Le Moine wondered. A survivor of Stalingrad during the great Russian war sharing his undaunted skill with the men he led. Why the questions about his father? A soldier his mother said was a Patriot who fought for his country. A soldier admired and remembered with great sorrow. A father Jacques could be proud of.

Sergeant Max's memory of SS Sturmbannführer Joachim Roth revived whenever he looked at Jacques's eyes, blonde hair, smile. Definitely a 'Blitz Baby'. A Franco-German love child.

For Sergeant Max, the savagery of the Vietnam war was only exceeded by the German Army's suffering in Russia, starving, freezing to death, attacked by Cossacks decapitating prisoners with swords. Sergeant Max recalled roads crowded with retreating trucks and horse-drawn wagons, despondent foot soldiers with blankets over their summer uniforms wearing Russian winter helmets, frozen boots wrapped in rags as they marched past the wounded and dying on the roadside pleading for help. Cripples who crawled like moaning animals begging for the mercy they never received on a 'Highway of Horror.'

Surviving on bowls of rice, drinking river water, housed like animals in Bamboo Cages flooded waist deep during Monsoon rains, Prisoners slept standing, embracing each other to keep from falling and drowning. Viet Minh guards tormented the defeated Europeans who were once their Masters, exploiting their land, violating their wives and daughters, burning their homes and villages, forcing Peasants to work as Slave Laborers on Colonial Rice and rubber Plantations.

9,000 French Prisoners died of disease and starvation. Three thousand survivors, abandoned by their Viet Minh guards, learning of the 1954 Geneva Accords, broke free of their cages and gathered their remaining strength to dance and cry and sing 'La Marseilles' as parachutes floated down from the sky bringing food and medicine. A futile nine year war ended illusions of a Colonial Empire killing thousands of Vietnamese who only wanted to be left alone to peacefully live traditional lives.

Divided into Communist North and democratic South Vietnam, promised free elections unifying their country, the Geneva Accord was a great victory for Ho Chi Minh's lifetime struggle to create a free and independent Vietnam.

One Million Catholics, hearing "Virgin Mary is going South," fled to the Provinces where government forces in Saigon welcomed them. No one could foresee the 21 years of destructive war needed to unite the 'Socialist Republic of Vietnam' in 1975.

SIX

Pain, shame, remorse -- can't do anything about what I feel Jacques Le Moine admitted, looking out at the sea from the rail of a Troopship repatriating French soldiers to France. "I've been participating in a Horror movie -- burning villages -- killing children -- watching legless beggars plead for charity when all we brought them was war without victory -- and now, ordered to Algeria to fight another lost cause, I bring more bombings, murder, torture and assassinations killing 'Freedom Fighters' struggling for independence. 'Ours not to reason why -- ours but to do or die!' wrote a poet who knew a soldier's life is doomed to betrayal by politicians who learn nothing from humiliating defeat. And Yes -- I will now engage in 'Rat Hunts' exterminating Algerians fighting for independence."

Jacques Le Moine, troubled by these thoughts, raised his arm to throw a piece of bread overboard feeding seagulls diving to catch food in mid-air. He shouted -- "Only birds know freedom, Sergeant Max, only birds."

Sergeant Max nodded, tossing more bread into the sea replying -- "Only birds are free. Only birds. We who fight where ever we are sent are called murderers, assassins, rapists when serving our nation. Like in Stalingrad, freezing in underground Bunkers, with blankets covering our summer uniforms to survive penetrating cold. Sheltered inside walls built of frozen corpses, we were a starving army in rags with no hope of rescue, with every wound a death sentence. Breaking out of our encirclement, fleeing across snow covered Steppes, was impossible. Betrayed by Generals fighting a war they knew they could not win, defeated by cold, rain, snow, mud and without roads to supply their armies, our

Leaders abandoned 90,000 soldiers at Stalingrad who cried when they remembered childhoods singing -- 'Silent Night -- Holy Night' on Christmas eve. Yes. Only birds are free. Only birds. And in 1953, after ten years as Slave Laborers, only five thousand of the ninety thousand who surrendered repatriated to Germany to rebuild their lives."

Jacques Le Moine recalled reading a famous author who wrote -- "Death and destruction is the language we speak in a world unable to learn from history. Doomed to repeat the past killing fifty million human beings we wonder -- can we ever prevent the horrors inflicted on all nations of all colors, creeds and ideologies? Forgetting the language of love and Justice, we destroy civilizations, ignoring International Law racing to disaster. Mothers singing -- 'I didn't raise my boy to be a soldier' -- are futile supplicants ignored by Leaders protecting their nation's interests. Fighting endless wars, seduced by our military power in an unholy alliance with the Devil, we hope to make the situation less bad."

Sergeant Max agreed -- "Malaya, Vietnam, Algeria and Indonesia are Colonialism's graveyards. In Germany Hitler Youth raised their arms saluting their Leader as they marched and sang and fought proclaiming superiority over all other races -- Fanatics serving 'The Wave of The Future' -- enslaved Europe, devastated great cities -- Warsaw, Rotterdam, Berlin, Dresden, Munich, Kiev, Stalingrad -- setting the world on fire not knowing how to extinguish the flames of hate and fear and political dogmas. Civilizations die by suicide -- not murder. They self-destruct -- and when German Generals recognized their guilt they attempted to overthrow the mad dog leading them, their crimes -- their moral failure could not be so easily redeemed. They were caught, convicted and hung knowing millions died at their command -- their legacy -- a dark page in history that can never be erased."

Jacques Le Moine turned from the rail remaining silent a moment before saying -- "Rats always leave a sinking ship. When our General's attempt to assassinate De Gaulle for supporting Algerian Independence failed, they fled, abandoning the Harkis, troops who fought for France. Now considered Traitors, Harkis were lynched, tortured and doused in petrol incinerated by patriotic Algerian Vigilantes. One million European settlers fled to France betrayed by their government after a futile war to retain their farms. The Harkis, transported to France, housed in miserable Internment Camps, denied the rights of French citizens, survived as low-paid agricultural workers."

As a defeated warrior, Jacques Le Moine did not celebrate Algerian Independence. His comrades, killed in futile wars, lived on with painful memories that would never vanish. No Victory Parade on the Champs Elysee, no Trumpets, no waving flags, no applause or cheers greeted humiliated French soldiers returning from Algeria and Viet Nam. Jacques Le Moine watched France fall into anarchy with one million students, workers, farmers, and intellectuals on strike in demonstrations occupying Paris, closing the government for several weeks. Alarmed by Police brutality, fearing another assassination, responding to chants of "Adieu De Gaulle, Adieu De Gaulle" -- the President fled to Germany. When assured of the Army's support, De Gaulle returned to France dissolving the National Assembly calling for a new election.

Discharged, seeking a quiet life with his mother in St. Agathe, Jacques Le Moine returned to consider his future. He had killed, witnessed torture, destroyed villages turning away from the suffering he had inflicted on helpless peasants. He asked -- was obeying orders war or murder? Would he feel remorse forever? Sleepless nights and long walks along lonely village roads did not ease the pain of surviving when so many good men died. Drinking and thinking in a Cafe every evening resolved nothing, he felt he was living half-way between life and death finding no answer to who am I? What am I? What will my future be ? And yes! Again and again. Who was my father?

A bundle of letters, tied with string, hidden in the bottom drawer of a bureau provided a revelation. Addressed to someone Simone claimed was his father, a French Prisoner of War were stamped: 'ADDRESSEE UNKNOWN -- RETURN TO SENDER.'

Jacques Le Moine read the letters describing the innocent joys of living in a Paris whose heart was forever young and gay, where defeat was acceptable, a bargain for the future of France. He asked his mother: "Why did you flee Paris?"

Simone explained: "I fled to St Agathe to escape 'Legal Purification' in a City gone mad, Patriots hungry for revenge tried to erase the shame and humiliation of the occupation. Naked, with shaved heads, women who had German Lovers were paraded in the streets, pelted with stones and excrement, some carrying Blitz babies in their arms. Writing letters supported my claim your father was French -- insuring I would escape the suffering of 'horizontal collaborators' -- as if true love between a man and a woman, regardless of nationality, was not possible."

Jacques Le Moine taking his mother's hand replied: "Everyone fights their own war. In their own way. We are all warriors." Simone nodded, saying -- "I did not know my beautiful Lover, Joachim Roth would later be tried and convicted as a War Criminal, guilty of unspeakable crimes. I never thought a good man could do evil asking -- is any man totally good?

And you, my son, what did you do in Vietnam and Algeria? Are you -- a good man -- innocent? Not knowing evil -- could you recognize what is good in all men and women? And tell me how the immorality of Hiroshima and Nagasaki differs from Auschwitz? Treblinka? Dachau? What good do we fight for in wars? What price do we pay to defend civilization? Guilt? Grief? Shame? Alcoholism? Despair? Suicide? Who in our mad world is good? -- who is Evil?" '

Sergeant Max found the answer to Simone's question on the snow covered steppes of Russia. Gravely wounded, left behind to die by his retreating Army, Sergeant Max awaited capture by advancing Russians. Floating in and out of consciousness, accepting inevitable death, he recalled being placed on a sled and dragged to a small Hut by an old Peasant women. Removing his frozen clothing, his Savior rubbed his legs and arms restoring life to his frozen limbs. Working slowly, tenderly, she seemed to be praying as she massaged his frozen flesh. Fed a bowl of hot soup, gently covered with a warm blanket, Sergeant Max slept for days and nights and awakening became aware of the old women's strength and courage as she held him in her arms, dressed and fed him, saving his life. He could not recall how many days or weeks the old woman sheltered him. He called her mother. She smiled, nodded, and replied in words he did not know but understood. She was not mad but grieving. He was her lost son restored to life.

The German Army regrouped, re-armed and re-fueled, counter-attacked the Russians re-taking the battlefield they had abandoned. Two SS Sonderkommandos entered the Hut, Sergeant Max identified himself explaining he was a battlefield casualty saved by this kind Peasant.

Unmoved by his story the SS men raised their rifles killing the old woman who fell to the floor like a broken bag of human flesh and blood and lost hope.

SEVEN

Who were those bodies hanging from a Gallows in the Village Square, wrists tied behind their backs, necks broken, faces distorted by death's final agony? A gruesome sight young Max avoided walking to school, ignoring signs on their shirts. They were Communists, Socialists, Jews, and sexual offenders, defilers of Aryan blood. They must be destroyed young Max agreed raising his arm, shouting the new German greeting -- Heil Hitler! -- Heil Hitler! -- parading holding a flaming torch led by a hundred beating drums arousing feelings of unlimited power. As a Hitler Youth, Max's destiny was to make Germany great again, to die so that Germany might live giving glory and purpose to his life.

Dancing around a flaming bonfire of books, shouting "Jews get out" -- young Max felt triumphant with every book he threw into the flames. Books corrupting Germany. Shakespeare. Plato. Heinrich Heine. Thomas Mann. Voltaire. Thomas Paine. Karl Marx. Books promoting a civilization that will soon vanish under the iron boot of Nazi Germany. Yes. The Triumph of the Will is inevitable young Max believed while high above Nuremberg a formation of Stuka Dive Bombers flew over the Stadium where ten thousand cheering Storm Troopers in regimental formations proclaimed -- "death before dishonor!" -- "One people! One Leader! One Reich!"

Working from lists provided by cooperative Jewish Councils, the Police rounded up Jews, cripples, mental defectives and all opponents of National Socialism in a brutal cleansing of Germany prohibiting Jews from Parks, swimming pools, Cinemas, and Universities in a pitiless program freeing Germany of non-Aryans. Fighting in France, Russia and Algeria young Max became a warrior. War his only profession with no future other than to kill, torture and ravage foreign countries. In Algeria he helped the French do to Algerians what Germany did in occupied France. In Vietnam Sergeant Max fought Insurgents struggling to be free of Colonial exploitation, hunger, disease and violent death. The "Wretched of the Earth" became Martyrs fighting for their dignity and freedom with massive street demonstrations, bombings, assassinations, and massacres of innocent bystanders evoking outrage, horror and the moral degradation and shame of torture. Meeting terror with greater terror, raining death on villages sheltering the enemy, sowing land mines making verdant farmlands unworkable, defoliating forests and Jungles, Sergeant Max fought an endless war on terror that almost destroyed his soul.

International Security Partners LLC, a Limited Liability Corporation listed on the NY Stock Exchange was formed by several retired Generals and international Security experts providing Mercenary soldiers to defend the political and economic interests of their Clients. Privatizing war -- making combat profitable -- ISP employed veterans who had no other profession than war. Well paid, with a reputation for brutality, they were 'war lovers' fighting on three continents ignoring the Rules of War uncontrolled by military Chains of Command. Often high on drugs, they became terrorists bringing death and destruction to non-combatants.

Sergeant Max now fought for anyone seeking military solutions to political problems. As a Mercenary Sergeant Max felt neither the pride or the honor of serving God and country as a patriotic duty. Fighting dirty wars for money -- he felt unclean. The line between war and murder vanished in pursuit of profit. Fighting small wars in failed states, Sergeant Max abandoned all thought of living a peaceful civilian life.

Jacques Le Moine visited Joachim Roth's grave, head bowed, struggling to understand feelings for a father he never met. They were warriors, defending conflicting ideologies testing whether freedom or slavery will prevail. His father, a War Criminal believed Aryans are Übermensch and violence the source of national greatness -- Jacques, a recipient of France's highest military honors dedicated to 'Liberty -- Equality -- Fraternity -- killed civilians in endless ideological wars.

Military cemeteries in Europe, Africa and Asia, rows of crosses, flowers, and engraved obituaries honoring the dead seemed haunted by ghosts who will never again hear song birds welcoming the dawn of a new day, or watch a glorious sunset's fading light reminding them life passes and all we ever possess is memory.

In a world burning with hatred -- with millions of Refugees fleeing their homelands -- Was 'Rest in Peace' possible?

EIGHT

Herb Howard believed wars most pitiful victims are children. No matter the doctrine, ideology, or patriotic purpose proclaimed by Dictators, Presidents, Prime Ministers, or the Pope, -- a good war is not possible. Wars fighting for God and Country, for a Nation's 'Manifest Destiny' -- or glory -- are tragedies killing millions of children. For children there is no honor in battlefield wounds, no Purple Hearts for lost legs, shattered arms, blinded eyes and death by starvation. No 'Body Count' records their loss buried in mass graves concealing our shame. We hide our guilt with patriotic speeches, military parades, erecting statues to our heroes as if there can ever be something heroic about killing children. We drop bombs. ravage cities, displace populations, commit genocide repeating war time horrors. We are all War Criminals -- and not protesting our savagery makes us complicit in murder.

Herb Howard shared Philosopher Bertrand Russell's statement -- "thought looks into the pit of hell and is not afraid --thought is great and swift and free and the light of the world and the chief glory of Man." -- and with confidence in his convictions -- Herb Howard became an active Pacifist.

On Easter Sunday, 1955, three hundred thousand demonstrators of the Campaign For Nuclear Disarmament converged on Trafalgar Square protesting importing Trident Missiles to the United Kingdom. Blocking London's streets for five days, students, workers, housewives, parents, bankers, lawyers, university professors and dignified businessmen wearing bowler hats and carrying rolled umbrellas demanded abolition of nuclear weapons. For four months anti-nuclear activists also blocked the entrance to a Missile Base in Scotland chanting -- "No More War" -- "Give Peace a chance" -- and -- "One World or None".

Herb Howard, in his RAF uniform, led several thousand veterans into Hyde Park -- some on crutches or in wheel chairs, or wearing dark glasses and walking with canes displaying their sacrifice for England. Chanting -- "Never Again!" -- "Never Again!" -- Herb Howard felt they were speaking Truth to Power, revolutionary voices that could not be denied. He felt the intoxicating surge of political energy attempting to overthrow a government. -- Mass demonstrations -- "Armies for Peace" -- were not an impossible dream but the only hope for ending recurring wars and the belief in military power. As a Veteran, Herb Howard discovered what he wanted to do with his life. Recalling Shakespeare's --"There is a Tide in the affairs of men which taken at the flood lead on to fortune".... Herb Howard determined to stand for Parliament.

Herb Howard's maiden speech envisioned world-wide demonstrations overthrowing corrupt governments failing to provide employment for young citizens who were homeless and unemployable without education and skills required to marry and raise families. He spoke of despair and violence, of starvation, of failed crops on dry barren lands becoming dust. He described floods and hurricanes, nature's destructive power driving millions from their homelands. He predicted without the wisdom to address these problems -- our future will be forfeit. The choices we make today -- will determine our tomorrow.

In Paris, in 1955, Jacques Le Moine fought Gendarmes brutally restoring 'Law and Order'. From the Arc de Triumph to the Place de Ville, the Champs Elysee filled with a hundred thousand anti-war demonstrators demanding resignation of a corrupt government sacrificing a hundred thousand French soldiers in Vietnam and Algeria to retain a morally bankrupt Colonial Empire. Breaking store windows, overturning cars, throwing fire bombs, attacking the police with sticks and pavement stones, mobs of angry demonstrators overwhelmed the Police with a rage continuing for several days and nights of uncontrollable fury.

Firing tear gas and live ammunition, the Police killed hundreds of students and workers throwing the wounded and the dead into the Seine to be carried out to sea uncounted but not forgotten.

French Generals could not forgive De Gaulle's granting independence to Algeria, a dishonorable betrayal of the Moslems who fought with the French to retain Algeria as a Department of France. French Colonials, the "Pied Noirs" talked of revolution while in Algeria the "Harkis", now considered traitors, were slaughtered by Algerian nationalists.

Jacques Le Moine viewed these events with divided loyalties. When General Massu's Paratroopers and Tanks surrounded Paris -- threatening a "Coup d' Etat" -- Jacques Le Moine resisted joining them as a million Parisians fled shutting down theaters, Cafes and the Metro. For 48 hours France watched and waited. Wondering -- "Can De Gaulle prevent another bloody French revolution?"

After two days Paratroopers returned to their Barracks, Tanks were withdrawn, and General Massu, leader of this demonstration of military power urged General De Gaulle to form a new government based on Peace and justice for all.

Hatred for De Gaulle persisted. Fanatics thought him a Dictator betraying the Republic's humanitarianism. Several failed assassinations de-stabilized France. Snipers fired at De Gaulle parading down the Champs Elysee and praying in Notre Dame. The hope De Gaulle could save France was threatened by a roadside ambush by three gunman leaving 14 bullet holes in his limousine. Unharmed, De Gaulle's reputation for being bullet proof unchallenged, the self-proclaimed President of 'New France' executed his assassins refusing clemency to Patriots who believed they were serving the Republic's best interest.

There was a time when 'Cannon Fodder' refused to be fed into the jaws of Death. During the mass slaughter of World War One, France sacrificed more than one million soldiers to prevent invading Germans from capturing Paris. Rushing re-enforcements to the front in taxis and buses, winning the Battle of the Marne, France survived despite mutiny and desertions where 27,000 conscripts fled the battlefields. 50 of 113 French Divisions refused to leave their trenches. Marching past their Generals, obedient troops, baaing like sheep, suffered 30,000 casualties in the first three hours of a ten day offensive killing a total of 120,000 in futile attacks against the devastating power of machine guns.

23,000 were convicted of Mutiny and sentenced to prison. 500 were sentenced to death. 49 executed. And promising no more offensives, and better food, and more rotations from the front, French Generals confidently awaited the arrival of Americans who certainly will bring victory.

President Woodrow Wilson in 1917 declared "it is a fearful thing to lead a great nation into war... defending the Right is more precious than Peace... Fighting to make the world safe for Democracy, America is privileged to spend her blood for the principals that gave her birth and happiness and the Peace she treasured... God helping her she can do no other."

In 1940 President Franklin D. Roosevelt justified America's entrance into WWII fighting for Freedom of speech, Freedom of Worship, Freedom from want and Freedom from Fear. A vital step on the long hard road to Freedom confirmed by the Atlantic Charter, the United Nations and the Universal Declaration of Human Rights.

No one goes to war alone. Nor can we calculate the damage to souls by the barbarisms of war. In the name of Patriotism, nations fight for land and glory ignoring the moral guilt of Leaders responsible for millions of civilian casualties. We 'disappear' the innocent in indefinite detention and torture unable to curtail the rising rate of suicide of Veterans overcome by guilt and shame. The self-inflicted wounds of war continue as each new generation brings their passionate Patriotism to the world's distant battlefields.

President De Gaulle refined the art of Political theater doing the unexpected, smashing the status quo, compelling the world to notice him. Proud, arrogant, a King in Exile, he disdained his unpopularity with 'Free World' leaders. Roosevelt loathed him. Churchill said he was the "heaviest Cross he had to bear" making no secret of his hatred for an expatriate Colonel who in four years transformed himself from a powerless "Free French" Pretender to a recognized world statesman. As President of liberated France, De Gaulle would often retreat to his private estate in Colombey for weeks of thought emerging to prevent Britain's membership in the European Economic Community, defeating hopes for a unified multi-lingual Europe without borders. President De Gaulle, ended the Vichy French government's humiliating compromises with Hitler enabling France to be recognized as a world power in 1945.

Confiding in his Aide, Charles De Gaulle observed -- "We are on the stage of a theater where, since 1940 I have been sustaining an illusion giving France the appearance of a solid, firm, confident and expanding country, while it is a worn-out nation, which thinks only of its comfort. I make people believe France is a great country, determined and united, while it is nothing of the sort. France is a worn-out country, made to be supine, not fight and win wars. That is how things are and I cannot do anything about it -- I keep the theater going as long as I can, and then -- after me -- have no illusion -- things will go back to where they were."

Winston Churchill disagreed saying: "From Stettin in the Baltic to Trieste in the Adriatic an Iron Curtain has descended across the continent of Europe. Our supreme task is to guard the homes of common people from the horrors and miseries of another war. The dark ages may return. The Stone Age may return while the gleaming wings of science may bring about our total destruction.

There is nothing our enemy admires so much as strength -- and there is nothing for which they have less respect than military weakness."

Jacques Le Moine knew he was being followed whenever he strolled St. Agathe's streets or roads. He was often depressed and tried to live a quiet life. He was not paranoid. Footsteps tailing him were as real as his love of France. Duty, Honor, Country remained his inviolable code of loyalty to France. His conscience was clear. He was a soldier rejecting politics.

After strolling thru the village Jacques Le Moine sat at a sidewalk Cafe drinking Cafe au lait, reading a newspaper, or watching passing street traffic. A tall gentleman wearing dark glasses raised his hat and asked permission to sit. Jacques Le Moine nodded setting aside his newspaper.

"Permit me to introduce myself," the Intruder said reaching across the table to hand Jacques Le Moine a card inscribed -- 'Chevaillier a la Table Rounde'.

"A Knight of the Round Table?" Jacques Le Moine replied reading the card. "Are you defending King Arthur?"

The Intruder smiled and laughed, leaned back in his chair explaining -- "We are Patriots fighting communism with Truth. With France, Italy, Germany and eastern Europe becoming Red, with political violence destabilizing society, with fear and despair spreading like cancer we defend democratic Europe recruiting Patriots who recognize who is destroying France. To save France from tyranny we must defeat De Gaulle."

"And you believe I can help?"

"Yes."

"You are mistaken. I'm only a soldier."

"True," the Intruder replied, "But even an ordinary soldier can save France. -- There is more than one way to fight for your country."

"Certainly not by assassination," Jacquess Le Moine replied.

The Intruder paused and then said -- "Truth is on the march -- and truth shall make you free! When the truth is known, when diabolic plots are revealed, when the sunlight of exposure lifts the darkness of deceit restoring confidence in our government, there will be no greater honor than fighting for freedom."

"I'm no Informer," Jacques Le Moine insisted. "And I would not want to defend your idea of freedom."

Jacques Le Moine felt the heart, like a compass, always knows the way home. His childhood with Nuns shattered his belief in God. And without God -- he was a warrior's son refusing to fight for ideologies promising neither war or peace but more street demonstrations, more tear gas, more fire-bombing, more killings, none worth dying for. During agonizing nightmares Jacques Le Moine, tormented and anguished, broke down the door of a Vietnamese village hut, throwing a grenade into a room crowded with women and children. Torching the hut, he went to the next one thinking this is no way to fight for freedom with bugles sounding Taps and the Chaplain reading the 23rd Psalm over unmarked graves as Vultures, sitting high in the trees flapped their wings as if mourning the dead. Jacques Le Moine felt overcome by pity and the sadness of a life troubled by killings staining his immortal soul. He recognized how he lost his childhood innocence in war, and now, as a moral outlaw felt unremitting shame saying -- "we are all children of the Holocaust, no one is without guilt for Europe's suicide, a disaster that can only be mitigated by fighting for freedom and decency, our duty in a world where lies become the foundation of governments. The death of religion, the outrages of nationalism, the break-down of International Law enhancing the power of Autocrats, made Europe's tragic fate inevitable. With protests in London, Paris, Berlin, New York and Prague, my voice is one of many striving for a better world. Our leaders have failed our young who demand more education, more jobs and the opportunity to raise families free of wars, famine, and terrorism. The alternative to the rule of law will be the destruction of civilization. Endless wars threatening the existence of life with famines, epidemics and international lawlessness recurring every generation. The lights are going out all over the world and I ask -- do we have the courage to light them again when the only language nation's speak is war? When Justice, and Truth no longer govern -- who are we -- what have we become as we struggle to survive? With Presidents excusing torture as the price of victory -- I ask what have we done to ourselves? Where is our pride? Our honor? Our protests are cries of despair fearing nothing will change, -- nothing will ever be right and decent again."

Writing to his unborn son Jacques Le Moine wrote: "You are my child of the future and will inherit a world in which life is too difficult for most people. Hopefully your life will be different from mine though the balance of good and evil will be the same. You will derive strength from every threat to your survival, each day a day of triumph and self-discipline, free from doubt. There should be no place in your life for self-pity, no time for despair, no room for fear. You will have much in common with others, hopes, compassion, understanding and the presence of a soul. You will learn hard work is a moral conquest safeguarding your spirit, protecting your existence. You will discover a moral stance can be more far-sighted than any other choice and what survives is -- love -- and the hard work of changing the world."

The Abbaye de Saint Cros is known for offering 'Retreats' to troubled souls, over-stressed businessmen, recovering alcoholics, and husbands seeking ten days of peace and quiet away from their wives and children. The Pere Hospitalier welcomed all strangers to the Abbaye saying: "Here you will pick up the shattered pieces of your life and regain command of your soul". Taking a vow of silence, living free of the confusions of newspapers and television, Jacques Le Moine went to the Abbaye hoping to find the peace and understanding he craved. He meditated in a Cell with a hard bed, a wash basin, a commode and a Prie-Dieu watched over by a Crucifix on the wall. Eating in silence, drinking bitter coffee from a soup bowl, chewing hunks of black bread, Jacques Le Moine sought a penance achieved by humble food, fasting and abstinence.

In a narrow alley leading to the kitchen door of the Abbaye de Saint Cros, a long wooden table set with bowls of hot soup, coffee and loaves of bread was prepared for a long line of homeless disabled veterans, beggars and cripples waiting patiently for the bell to ring and the noonday meal served. Giving bread to the hungry, Jacques Le Moine felt humbled witnessing the suffering of men who had nothing in life but faded memories of parents, brothers, sisters, wives and children. Defeated by poverty and disease they silently lived barren lives with every meal a victory over death. Feeding them, sustaining their struggle, recognizing their humanity, seemed noble and honorable giving greater purpose to Jacques Le Moine's troubled life.

NINE

As a boy Sergeant Max remembered when half of German workers were unemployed with homeless citizens waiting at soup kitchens for a loaf of bread. Crippled decorated Veterans begged for pennies. Poverty and despair were everywhere with sullen anger at the economic failures of the 'Jew government' all true Germans despised. Bank failures, Bankruptcy, suicides, violent crimes and a breakdown in civil behavior seemed an inevitable part of Germany's future. The penalty of defeat in the first World war. Then, on January 30th 1933, as Adolph Hitler became Chancellor and President, Germany was reborn with his promise of a 'Thousand Year Reich.' 'Deutschland Uber Alles' became possible. Thousands, and then hundreds of thousands and then millions responded to Hitler's cry -- "Germany Awake!" Intoxicated, shouting Sieg Heil!, Germans followed Torch lit parades with Battalions of Brown shirts marching in the streets. Brass Bands played every afternoon for War Veterans wearing decorations. Loudspeakers broadcast Hitler's voice heard wherever you walked. With horns blaring, trucks raced down the avenues carrying Storm Troopers shouting Death to Jews! Radios broadcast Hitler's voice to 6 million homes and at Nuremberg Rallies twenty thousand Nazis shouted Sieg Heil! honoring war dead by singing the Horst Wessel song, chanting 'out with old -- in with the New', applauding the defeat of the criminal Weimar government, cheering the death of Democracy replaced by --'Work Family Fatherland' and -- 'Order Authority The Nation'. "Oh how good it was to be alive in New Germany," Sergeant Max remembered. "How good to be a heroic page in German History as Dirigibles flew Swastikas across oceans and the eyes of the world focused on Hitler. What will Hitler do now? the world wondered, fearing another war."

Defying his parents, politically conservative devout Lutherans, Sergeant Max enlisted in the Hitler Youth to help make Germany great again.

In France, Daniel Cohn Bendit, also known as Danny the Red, was a Warrior who never fired a gun. Words were his weapon. Passionate speeches inciting ten million French workers, students and farmers in May, 1968 to demonstrate against their government. Eight hundred thousand marched through Paris where students fought Policemen brutally attempting to restore law and order. When President Charles De Gaulle called Danny The Red -- "a German Jewish Traitor who should be expelled as a seditious alien" demonstrators replied -- "We are all German Jews".

In New York, Chicago, Mexico City, Antwerp, Warsaw and Prague, demonstrators proclaimed a young generation's passionate opposition to governments fighting wars in Vietnam and Algeria.

In Berlin, on June 1961, 19,000 East Berliners fled Communist East Germany to live in the democratic West. Doctors, Engineers, and skilled mechanics were an unacceptable 'Brain Drain' fleeing a ruthless Police state. A concrete barrier topped with barbed wire, the Berlin Wall 'anti-fascist bulwark' attempted to stem the mass defections crippling a struggling communist economy. For the next 28 years two million East Germans climbed over the wall crashing thru check points in cars, crawling thru sewers to escape a ruthless dictatorship. On November 9th 1989, accepting the victory of mass demonstrations, the gates to freedom were opened to a wave of delirious Germans, dancing and singing armed with picks and hammers tearing down a hated symbol of political oppression.

For eight months in 1968, attempting to democratize a nation Prague's 'Spring of freedom' witnessed a massive rebellion of students, workers and shopkeepers fighting for freedom of conscience, speech, independent Trade Unions, and an end to government corruption and incompetence. Led by Alexander Dubcek opposing an invading army of 600,000 soldiers armed with tanks, machine guns and tear gas, they defended his attempt to establish "Communism with a human face", Freedom Fighters fought and died for their dreams of justice and human dignity.

Certainly the cry for freedom is without borders. In 1980, in Gdansk, Poland, inspired by Prague's "Velvet Revolution", 16,000 Polish shipyard workers demanding free Unions made one more brave step toward liberty, justice and equality in Eastern Europe. Led by Lech Walesa, supported by workers, intellectuals, and the Catholic Church, the protestors formed 'Solidarity', a free and independent Trade Union guaranteed freedom of speech, printing, publishing and release of political prisoners. Solidarity's victory inspired a wave of work stoppages throughout Poland and political unrest in other Soviet satellites, later bringing down the USSR when Premier Gorbachev was unwilling to use force to suppress all hopes for democracy in Eastern Europe.

On June 4th, 1989, in Beijing's Tiananmen square, one million protesters gathered around the Goddess of Democracy statue, a replica of the Statue of Liberty, protesting one party rule. Similar demonstrations in Shanghai and other cities evoked a brutal government response by 10,000 soldiers employing Tanks, live ammunition and clouds of tear gas. Demonstrating in front of 'The Gates of Heaven", China's most revered Shrine, waving flags and banners proclaiming their demands, students set fire to tanks, threw stones and bricks at soldiers, dancing and singing revolutionary songs in an intoxicating ecstasy threatening to overturn the basic doctrines of a Communist police state.

Emerging from the crowd, a young unarmed student confronted the line of tanks entering the square, the demonstrators silently watching as he blocked the path of the invading tanks, raising his arms, halting their relentless threat. The rumbling roar of a hundred diesel engines suddenly ceased as the tanks stopped, the demonstrators cheering the student's courageous and solitary act of defiance. Yes indeed. One man made history.

The son of German Jewish refugees who fled Hitler, Danny The Red lived in France until 1945 when the family returned to their abandoned German home. Danny avoided the French Army draft by registering as a German citizen. With dual citizenship, fluent in German and French, Danny became the outstanding European voice opposing war crimes like torture, renditions, and Regime changes. Closing the 'Metro' and railroads in Paris, burning cars, breaking store windows, building barricades and singing 'La Marseillaise', protestors led by Danny re-enacted a revolutionary tradition beginning with the fall of the Bastille in 1787 and the Paris Commune massacres in 1870. The paralyzed French government met violence with violence, with Danny The Red leading a new generation of 'Freedom Fighters' demanding living wages, more jobs, improved education, health care, and larger pensions as the price for restoring Law and Order.

Napoleon's historic victories inspired Danny's belief in a unified Europe. Standing on a chair to be seen by an audience, Danny raised both arms speaking to demonstrators waving flags and banners on Paris's grand avenues. Danny's childhood memories, wearing a yellow star, seeing Kristallnacht's broken windows convinced him Jews had no future in Germany. Hitler's speeches pledged their destruction while many Germans predicted he will soon be rejected for Germany is too civilized to tolerate his hatreds. "The Holocaust was a secret," Germans explained. "We did not think such an atrocity possible. Germans are not Barbarians. We are Europe's most civilized nation with the world's greatest Universities, most famous artists, philosophers and writers" Germany boasted as smoke rose from the crematoriums of Auschwitz, Belzak and Sobibor. As mountains of human ashes grew higher, forty foreign governments refused Jews sanctuary. "Yes!" Danny said -- "It will happen again" recalling March 30

1943 when 78,000 French Jews were transported to Auschwitz while the World watched Hitler's 'Final solution of the Jewish problem' being realized.

"In a nation without honesty, humility, seriousness, decency, morality and courage France has become a country that can only be loved with a broken heart," Danny shouted. "With the dilapidation of democracy, the breakdown of world order, and the ascendency of nationalism, capitalism, rule by corporations, special interests and the wealthy, France has entered the age of the undoing of international law, and universal truth."

TEN

Sergeant Max knew how to wait for a 'Subject of High Interest'. Sitting at a sidewalk Cafe drinking coffee, reading a newspaper or watching the passing crowd were part of his job working for International Security Partners whose customers always received what they contracted for -- kidnapping, extortions, and assassinations by Mercenaries fighting small wars. With cities paralyzed by street demonstrations demand for their services seemed unlimited. Snatching Danny The Red would prevent more violence, defeating De Gaulle and preventing establishment of authoritarian France.

"Danny's disappearance must appear accidental," Sergeant Max instructed his 'Hit team.' "Pedestrians are injured every day by taxis, buses and vans. So why not little Danny who is only five feet tall? Our Client is a wealthy Patriot financing spies, informers, embezzlers and drug dealers. We do whatever he asks. Make a snatch and go on to our next contract singing -- "Adieu De Gaulle! Adieu!" -- opposing an old Fart pretending he and not the Americans liberated France. Many Frenchmen believe Germany's surrender was no victory for freedom but a defeat of western civilization.

Danny entered the Cafe and sat at a sidewalk table. Glancing at his watch, he looked around the room as I approached identifying myself holding a Paris Soir in my hand. Danny looked up, smiled and said "Bonjour." I nodded my reply as two men emerged from a taxi waiting at the curb and grabbing Danny forced him into the cab with a hand covering his mouth silencing his protest. No one in the Cafe noticed a Snatch executed with such military precision."

Paris had several 'Safe Houses' and 'Black sites' run by governments to house Agents and interrogate 'Subjects of High Interest' kidnapped to influence elections. In a Europe ravaged by wars and political instability, 'Safe Houses' were an entrance into an Underground where information was acquired by sleep deprivation and bribery disclosing many 'Top Secrets' during the Cold War.

Ville Juif, Located 7 kilometers from the Arc de Triumph, founded in 1119 by Pope Callixtus to house Jews expelled from Paris, also had a 'Safe House', a renowned Cancer Research Institute, and a Psychiatric hospital used to house detainees.

Danny was held in a room with a bed, chair, wash basin and a commode. Looking out the window he saw a courtyard wet from a rainstorm reflecting sun light breaking thru clouds floating overhead and Danny wondered -- where was he? Who were his captors? Why was he here? He turned from the window, lay down on the bed covering himself with a blanket. Closing his eyes he attempted to sleep hoping to never again dream of being brutally interrogated, screaming, struggling to remain silent, his body aflame with pain.

When he awoke the Intruder was sitting next to his bed smoking a cigarette. Danny recalled waiting for him at the Cafe, reaching out to shake his hand. Who was this man? What did he want? Who was he working for? Danny's 'Enemy's List' included Vichy officials who will never forgive Americans for Liberating France and driving them from power. Was he being detained because he filled Paris with crowds rejecting rule by fear, distrust, hate and violence? With a Government opposing Freedom with tear gas and bullets, with drug abuse and suicides vanquishing hope, what France has become was described by Yeats, an English Poet writing -- 'Things come apart. The Center will not hold. The best lack all conviction while the worst are filled with a passionate intensity.'

"We must find a European solution to European problems," Danny argued. "Nationalism and border closings and forever wars cannot save nations incapable of compromise."

"Today is the day," Danny continued, "When my generation says -- stop lying to us -- stop killing us -- stop crippling us - stop driving us insane -- stop making families mourn our meaningless death fighting wars that cannot be won. Stop bringing our soldiers home in body bags -- crippled -- suicidal -- addicted to drugs -- forgotten -- insulted -- homeless. There is no glory in war. There is no "Just War" despite what we are told. "Why do you fear democracy," Danny continued. "Why do you make dissent a crime?"

The Intruder did not hesitate replying -- "We defend what you are destroying with fire bombs and mass hysteria. We fight for Law and Order establishing nations where loyalty to country and God rely on Ballots and not bullets to maintain civilization while refusing sanctuary to immigrants who will never become citizens."

"You encourage injustice," Danny replied. "Elite schools, well paid jobs and lucrative careers for people with snob voices while low salaries, high rents and taxes for other citizens are accepted without protest. Resisting change evokes our anger as we cry -- All Power to the People! -- Yes! -- someday there will be -- All Power to the People!"

"An impossible dream!" the Intruder replied. "I sow anger and fear corrupt elections aborting democracy with 'Regime Changes' crippling economies. What occurred in Viet Nam I repeated in Iraq and Afghanistan destroying cultural traditions, intensifying tribal conflicts, making the land barren, compelling millions to flee to countries where they are unwelcome. I am a virus of hate crossing borders, infecting everyone regardless of race, color or creed. I am the future where chaos becomes normal, where fear and despair are epidemic, where ignorance, bigotry and greed divide nations having no other purpose than maintaining military and economic power. Wherever I intrude -- I leave a wasteland of hate, fear, resentment and mass violence. Extremism is no vice when destroying democracy where the pursuit of happiness becomes rapacious greed. I am welcomed by corrupt Dictators. I am a destructive force energized by moral failure. A reality of homeless citizens searching for a homeland where they can live, work, and raise their families. Bomb battered cities become crowded Refugee Camps housing despair, disease and suicide for when hope vanishes, abandoning starving children becomes a heartless choice. To be or not to be?" becomes an existential questions millions ask in a world where all are victims of history."

Awakening from a deep sleep, pounding his head against the wall of his padded cell the Intruder shouted -- "give me liberty or give me death!" -- Then, exhausted, he rolled over in bed and dreamt of future glory going to war with an all-volunteer army fighting futile battles where all choices lead to the grave. Ignorant of history the Intruder repeated failed military solutions to the world's intractable problems creating unlimited 'Body Counts'.

"The Intruder's descent into madness was inevitable," wrote his Psychiatrist in an article published in a prestigious Medical Journal. "Declaring Mission Accomplished, the Intruder created his own reality based on self-serving intelligence devoid of truth. Unable to sustain his alternative vision of the world, the Intruder speaks an incoherent language of disassociated thoughts emerging from an undisciplined mind consumed by fear of failure. He talks in superlatives. Terrific, unbelievable, fantastic and magnificent describe achievements made possible by what he believes is his superior brain. A self-declared genius he relies on his instincts to make choices, to differentiate between right and wrong. For the King can do no wrong as he leads nations ever deeper into the quagmire of forever wars. There is no bright, shiny light at the end of the tunnel of darkness and hate he initiates. The Intruder intrudes -- and millions die."

"I am on God's side," the Intruder insisted. "God is with me! -- My voice influences politicians, journalists, and editors, defeating Peace Advocates by infiltrating governments with money. I corrupt elections rescuing nations from bankruptcy and despair. I serve millions eager to follow a leader guiding them on the path to greatness.

It is a grave responsibility sending young men to war. I hate war! Hate the chaos and casualty lists, hate the Peaceniks chanting outside my window -- "how many kids did you kill today?" -- as if I had no feelings for mothers, fathers, wives and children of the dead. As God is my witness I cannot sleep at night asking myself -- Why me? -- Why have I been chosen to save Freedom? I drop bombs for Peace devastating nations confident that violence in defense of Freedom is no vice.

That's who I am. I am the farmer and the banker, the rich man and the poor, the housewives and the husbands, factory workers, waiters, truck drivers, mechanics, immigrant laborers, and the unemployed. That's who I am! And what I believe is true as I guide nations into the future. Yes! I am who I am! --While many insist -- I am insane.

But No! What is insane is repeating past failures, stoking fear, hatred, anger and racial conflict eradicating the customs unifying society. A moral breakdown caused by forever wars, famines, population transfers, financial disasters and the despair from which we all flee. And yes. I can destroy the world."

ELEVEN

*"First they came for the socialists, and I did not speak out—
Because I was not a socialist.
Then they came for the trade unionists, and I did not speak out—
Because I was not a trade unionist.
Then they came for the Jews, and I did not speak out—
Because I was not a Jew.
Then they came for me - and there was no one left to speak for me."*

Sergeant Max struggled to understand how Martin Niemöller, a decorated officer in the first World War as a patriotic Lutheran Pastor opposed Hitler's racial science of mass extermination of Jews. Sentenced to solitary confinement at Dachau in 1937, liberated by Americans in 1945, Pastor Niemöller became a Pacifist advocating recognition of Germany's collective guilt and crimes against humanity. How did a war hero become a traitor? An advocate of world peace? Questions Sergeant Max often considered when considering his future.

Sergeant Max, A Hitler Youth in the notorious Adolf Hitler SS Panzer division, then a Legionnaire, and a Mercenary soldier, received orders he could not obey. -- "Elimination with extreme prejudice" meant murdering Danny The Red and Sergeant Max was a professional soldier -- not a murderer.

"There comes a time," Sergeant Max confided in his war diary, "When killing an enemy kills something within yourself. There is a moment when another death becomes unacceptable and battlefield insanity consumes both the victorious and the defeated. Casualties become a recurring catastrophe devastating each generation. I cried no more war knowing wars are inevitable bringing death and destruction to millions. -- I could not again shout -- One People! One State! One Leader! -- I could not raise my arm saying Heil Hitler! Heil Hitler! seeing the rubble that were once great cities, starving families dying in underground caves, walking skeletons begging for food, rotting corpses fouling the air. Hitler's 'thousand year Reich' became a land of death and despair. Yes. Indeed! Germans did this to ourselves. And certainly Pastor Niemöller was correct demanding we plead guilty to our war crimes, accept our collective guilt, experience redemption at the moment when a man must stake his life on the outcome of hard choices. Backing down from this existential challenge, a man's life and his nation are no more than piss water.

Remembering Pastor Niemöller -- I knew I could never kill Danny The Red."

The River Seine, flowing 483 miles from Paris to Le Havre, is navigable for 75 miles by ocean going ships docking at Rouen. For centuries, barges transported produce from fertile agricultural provinces to markets essential to French prosperity. The Seine also carried invaders, outlaws and dissenters fleeing tyranny. -- Like Emil Zola proclaiming -- "The Truth is on the March" -- as he fled to England to continue demanding justice for Captain Dreyfus. Danny's flight to England confirmed the belief -- 'History repeats itself, first as tragedy, then as Farce.'

Moored on the banks of a small creek flowing into the Seine, a floating village of Houseboats and Barges sheltered Parisians seeking escape from the city's political turmoil. They were writers, artists, journalists and students enjoying low rents and freedom pursuing the dreams and expectations inspiring their Bohemian lives. Sergeant Max's Houseboat "Invictus" was his retreat from a vagabond career, a refuge where he could think and read and understand what he must do to redeem and give meaning to his brutal destructive past. Deciding to save Danny's life, Sergeant

Max detained him aboard his Houseboat to flee to England. Travelling at night to avoid the Police, mooring on river banks from dawn to sunset, they saw homeless vagrants on the shore surviving in shacks of plywood and flattened tin cans. Draft Dodgers and Collaborators fleeing retribution, or Black Market Profiteers hiding their shame, or sadistic Policemen escaping War Crimes Trials. They were an illegal underworld without residence permits and jobs living half-way between life and brutal death by alcoholism, suicide, theft or murder.

"They are the trash of De Gaulle's New France," Danny commented.

"The waste product of a sick society," Sergeant Max agreed."

"We chanted -- 'Make love -- not war' and were tear-gassed," Danny replied.

"You can't change the world with demonstrations." Sergeant Max argued.

"Or with brutality," Danny said. "Break heads and you divide society into haves and have-nots, the entitled and the disenfranchised, with rage and fear waving Red flags over street barricades. We voted with the bodies now floating down the Seine."

"When dissent leads to violence, tragedy is inevitable," Sergeant Max replied. "The more History seems to change, the more it remains the same old story of wasted lives and inevitable death."

On the second day they encountered a vagrant refugee resting under a canvas tarp watching them moor to the river bank. A young girl, her head shaven, shivering under a blanket barely covering her desperate misery. A frightened animal, Danny thought, inviting her aboard, offering her bread and coffee. Hesitant, anxious, Monique silently accepted food raising the cup to her mouth as if receiving a sacrament. Scabs on unhealed wounds, missing teeth and a blood-stained dress revealed she had been brutally beaten. -- "Yes," she said -- "this is what French

Patriots did to me. Tore my dress. Shaved my head. Paraded me naked thru mobs screaming hatred and contempt for someone whose only crime was falling in love with a German soldier. Hypocrites! Tormenting women to wash away the shame of their defeat and collaboration with the Boche. Cowards who became heroic Freedom Fighters only when the Americans landed. Yes! France lost its soul during the occupation and beautiful France is gone forever!

What I want, I will never have," Monique continued. "I have always been what I am. Without education or a career, taught by Nuns to be a Bride of Christ, an object of men's insatiable lust, nothing more than a good fuck. I wanted a husband and family, watching my children grow, and grow old with the respect and dignity of a life well-lived. But not in France. Not in France governed by stupid, greedy, vain fools struggling for power, willing to pay any price to achieve their pathetic ambitions. Women are alone in France. All alone by the telephone waiting to be called by lovers who go off to wars they are incapable of winning. Their defeat, the occupation, an unbearable humiliation, a shameful revelation of who they are as men. Cowards. Cheering and singing and dancing as they surrendered their guns to invaders who were astonished by their Blitzkrieg victory. Surviving as Prisoners of war Frenchmen will return to repeat the mistakes of the past bringing more misery and despair to their defeated country. Vive La France! became a mournful lament at the grave of a once great nation.

And with the loss of our respect. men became violent to the one enemy they could defeat. Women! The Germans, tall, handsome lonely boys, like Olympic athletes, showed us consideration we could not refuse. We were hungry for tenderness, romance, the touch of a loving hand. We fell in love. Madly deeply in love with soldiers we admired and respected. Revenge! The Purification of France, became an orgy of fury attempting to wash away the shame of defeat. I can never forgive or forget the cruel faces, the curses, the contemptuous fury of people throwing excrement at young girls who followed their hearts into the arms of a lover."

Travelling at night, Sergeant Max observed the Constellations overhead with moonlight reflecting on the river illuminating the highway to freedom. Breath-taking beauty he ignored following other roads in Russia, France, and Algeria, and he wondered was this his final journey? Was he only a pathetic fugitive fleeing to England?

Or was he breaking away from a life devoted to violence? He somehow felt as if the hands of destiny, or perhaps a God he never believed in had reached out and touched something within his tormented soul. As a fugitive refusing to kill Danny, he was defining himself as someone who saving one life saves the world. Mooring the next morning on the river bank, they were greeted by a deserter from the Militia asking to come aboard. Hungry. unshaven, fleeing retribution for the atrocities he had committed during the occupation, he was a casualty in a time of revenge, the 'Purification' of all choosing the losing side in an ideological war. A time when many believed Liberation was a betrayal of all Marshall Petain fought for. A time of Trials, accusations, executions and Patriots thrown into Prisons. A time when the Pope asked Amnesty for all who fought the anti-Christ remaining faithful to the teachings of the Church. "We did our duty fighting the Reds raping their way across Europe," the Milicicn said. "We had no choice but to defend all that was good and true in our beloved France. We fought Jew government Ministers becoming wealthy while French Patriots starved in German Labor Camps. We failed to kill De Gaulle, the traitor who betrayed our great Marshall who fought to restore French honor and pride. I regret nothing I did to save Europe from Asiatics who would destroy civilization making citizens slaves to barbaric governments. As God is my witness I would kill Communists for Christ again and again to restore the soul of France.

I joined the Militia to fight the Reds and keep the Noirs from turning French cities into black slums of crime. filth and disease. Like Jews they spoiled everything good, true and beautiful in France. Our enemy were the Deputies, Ministers and De Gaullists betraying our beloved Marshall Petain's efforts to rebuild a France faithful to Church, Family and a glorious heritage that will never be replaced by the filth flooding Europe from the East. Making France great again became a holy Crusade without pity for all opposing our mission. Our Round-ups and executions restored the health of a nation. Our casualties were sacrifices on the altar of Freedom, blessed by the Church, and forgiven by the Pope for doing our duty no matter how hard. We were soldiers of Christ compelled to flee judgment by War Crimes Trials conducted by the true enemies of France. Reds. Blacks. And Jews."

On the fourth morning, mooring for the day on the river bank, Sergeant Max and Danny were greeted by an arm-waving Refugee shouting "Bonjour" welcoming their arrival. Shivering like a water-soaked dog, wet clothes clinging to his body, he appeared to have just emerged from the river. "Bon jour" he said again. "I am in distress and in need of a Savior. I assure you I did not swim for pleasure. I was thrown overboard by bastard Bargemen who did not welcome my company. Take me with you and I will tell of my adventures. How like the Wandering Jew I will never reach my destination but continue my endless journey to nowhere. Nowhere will I find peace. I fled Germany seeking sanctuary in France. Without a residence Permit or Work Papers, I have no choice but to flee to England praying they will welcome me. England, they say, is run by Jews who rule the world. Perhaps London is the new Jerusalem? Yes? In France, Liberty, Equality and Fraternity are only cries of what might have been had France fought on like England and not collaborated with Hitler who lives in the corrupted souls of Patriots. France will forever be haunted by the faces of 78,000 men, women and children sent to gas chambers with the smoke of a hundred Crematoriums flowing back to Paris carried on the winds of God's judgment blowing from the east. I pity France. "Apres Moi Le Deluge" your King said. After me the deluge! And that is what I am fleeing. The confusion, the division, the wanton homicidal stupidity of a nation changing governments every six months with all parties sharing a political Death Wish leading only to more carnage. More despair. Vive La France, people say.... Long Live France!... I don't think that is possible... Do you?"

On the fifth night travelling down the Seine, the Houseboat ran into what seemed to be driftwood floating on the current. Sergeant Max reached out with an oar to fend off a small boat occupied by a rower asleep, his head pillowed on a leather bag. Sergeant Max pulled the boat alongside as the rower awoke and handing the bag to him said, "Merci beaucoup! Take care!" Climbing aboard the House boat the rower added, "I am happy for your help, it seems I am tired of rowing. In fact, I am exhausted."

'You're lucky you were not run down by a Barge," Sergeant Max replied. "Rowing at night. No one could see you."

"Sad but true," said the rower. "But sometimes it is necessary to risk everything for a higher cause."

"And what is that cause?"

"Freedom!" the rower replied passionately. "Freedom! A cause worth dying for, don't you think?"

"Yes," Sergeant Max agreed. "Freedom is scarce in new France."

"Well said!" the rower replied. "Well said! Am I correct thinking you travel only at night when the Gendarmes are in bed with their wives and avoiding them is possible. Yes? For me, this journey is a question of life or death."

"A hard choice," Sergeant Max replied.

The rower smiled. "But not impossible for men of courage. France has many such men fighting to save her soul. Perhaps you are one?"

"Who are you?" Sergeant Max asked. "Where are you from? Where are you going?"

"I'm from everywhere where citizens yearn to be free. And where I am going is for you to decide."

"With luck, Rouen and the English Channel in two days."

"Allow me to travel with you. You will be well paid."

Sergeant Max hesitated before replying, asking himself, was the rower a mad man or a fool? Many Frenchmen, humiliated, shamed by occupation and defeat, betrayed by corrupt leaders, escape into suicidal delusions, depression and fury, desperate inmates fleeing an insane asylum. Perhaps taking one more fugitive would be one too many?

"I have no home in France," the rower explained. "Without papers I am homeless as a bird without a tree to land on. Homeless as a fish without a sea to swim in. Homeless as a Peasant without land to farm and feed his family. You might say I am Mr. Everyman. My middle name is tragedy, one of many unfortunate souls ruined by Europe's mass suicide. I must flee this tragic continent and find refuge where I can live in freedom because I want to truly live before I die. Tell me, is that too much to ask?"

> *"Means and ends on Earth*
> *Are so entangled that changing*
> *one changes the other too.*
> *Each different path brings*
> *other ends in view."*

During their river journey, Sergeant Max often wondered:

"Does a worthy end justify criminal acts to achieve that end? Does saving a million lives justify obliterating Dresden, Hiroshima, and Nagasaki? Is destroying European cities to liberate them rational? Is war's mass insanity inevitable?"

Sergeant Max questioned what he had become. Euro-trash creating political chaos, violating borders, defying laws to meet a Client's sordid ambitions, Fleeing France's destructive violence, Sergeant Max asked: "Was saving Danny an act of redemption seeking absolution beyond the power of a Priest? Forgive me Father for I have sinned were words that lost their meaning when I was ten. War is corrupting, corroding the soul, tarnishing the spirit with no heart unstained in a chaotic world unregulated by law in which good and evil, beautiful and ugly and the darkness of death prevail. There are people dedicated to evil, and without their example how could we recognize good? Dedication to evil, knowing it as evil, loving it as evil is prevalent in human beings who appear normal. The dice of God are loaded and for everything I missed in life I gained something else in a world in which not every secret is told, not every crime punished, not every virtue rewarded, not every wrong redressed while not seeing one's evil kills conscience. We are all one, we all create a God who will save us, and certainly how one dies and what one dies for defines the man."

TWELVE

Ghosts haunt Omaha beach where miles of sand extend as far as the eye can see with waves arriving unchanged since man first landed on this shore. Soaring overhead in a clear blue sky, mournful cries of seagulls offer lamentations for the men who fought and died here for what they believed. Veterans, and families of the dead kneel and pray at rows of crosses showing respect and love for brave men who sacrificed their lives that others may live. The American Military Cemetery at Omaha beach provides perpetual reverence to sacred memory.

Omaha Beach also collects the flotsam and wreckage of a crowded sea traversed by Freighters and Ferries discharging sewage and crude oil polluting a pristine shore.

On Omaha beach the body of Sergeant Max washed ashore holding a Journal containing his final message to the world he loved and lost.

"Tomorrow we arrive at the English Channel," Sergeant Max wrote. "Hope to safely cross treacherous waters where giant tankers run down small vessels without stopping for survivors. May God guide our Houseboat to the white cliffs of Dover, our beacon of hope, freedom's last sanctuary in Europe. We are a ship of fools dreaming of a better world that can never be achieved until a fundamental change in human behavior occurs. Fear, hatred, greed, lies and the lust for power have brought centuries of wars, famines and mass suicides. Man was not made to live in peace. An undeniable truth we must not ignore.

Monique dreams of a peaceful life with love, marriage and children escaping the turmoil and hatreds of France. In England she would become a woman, proud, independent, and loved. Yes. Loved. Not an impossible dream remembering her troubled past. Disappointing Lovers. Expectations never realized. Hopes unfulfilled. There must be more to her life than heartbreak, depression, suicidal thoughts. Always alone, with no one man in her life. No one man. No child. No life to call her own. Only what God made her. A piece of Adam's bone."

"Safe in England, the Millicien would escape tormenting nightmares leaving him exhausted, trembling when he awoke. Dreaming he saw four Jews, eyes closed as they prayed, swaying back and forth in an ancient ritual promising eternal life. In his dream he killed them, heads bowed, standing, refusing to fall as he continued shooting in a nightmare that would never free him from the horrors he perpetrated. Herding Jews into Cattle cars. Raping young girls. Tearing infants from a mother's arms. Shaving beards. Obeying orders in wild orgies of hate arousing the lust of power. The mad pleasure evoking fear in the helpless.

And when asked, Danny the Red replied what he wanted was: "More! More jobs, more education, more health care, higher pensions. Today is the day to create a nation where dissent is no longer a crime insuring Europe's suicide will never happen again. Yes! Never again will we remain silent watching the destruction of all we loved. Now is the time for all brave men to risk everything they have for a better world for our children."

And the Wandering Jew said: "The time of Martyrs may be come again and I will never find Peace in the undoing of a world consumed by death wishes. There will be another deluge after I vanish overthrowing all that is decent determining if mankind can survive another Holocaust. With belief in the divine in man rejected, I am at the end of the road on my march through history. I've arrived at the final page in the book of my life. I endure and pray with hope in my heart for enlightenment. After me -- only God knows what will happen."

And Mr. Everyman replied: "I hope to influence fate. I have no home where I can live in Freedom before I die. Failure. Success... I must be the difference I guess... Tell me... Am I asking too much?"

"Walking wounded," Sergeant Max wrote in his journal now at the National Archives in Washington. "A cargo of hopes and dreams, of lives struggling to survive searching for meaning. Can a society be invincible? Are we all lost souls where nations rise and fall in an endless parade of human folly? Can we escape the kinship of being human when all that survives is -- love?"

Judged mentally competent, stable and healthy by a team of renowned Psychiatrists, the Intruder, released from hospital, was elected President of the United States of America!

In his Inaugural Address the Intruder said:

"My Fellow Americans, in four years you will not recognize the Divided States of America, a nation enjoying Freedom to hate, Freedom to lie, Freedom to shoot and Freedom to insult anyone of a different language or color. In four years our beloved country will regain its God-given greatness with unlimited greed and privileges for the few and economic exploitation of all without education, health, job skills and the opportunity to live a better life. Free of all foreign entanglements, we will enjoy the greatest wealth and prosperity ever achieved by man. We will have lifted the burden of government regulations and a free press infecting our nation with Fake News.

Defining Truth will make us free to continue our long march into a history where will survive the hostility of the colored World. So I say to you, my beloved countrymen --The State of our nation is great!"

Thomas Paine wrote in 'The America Crisis' -

"These are the times that try men's souls:
the Summer Soldier and the Sunshine Patriot will in this crisis, shrink from the service of his country; but who stands by it now; deserves the love and thanks of man and women. Tyranny like Hell is not easily conquered; yet we have this consolation with us, that the harder the conflict, the more glorious the triumph."

In his second Inaugural address President Abraham Lincoln said:

"With Malice toward none, with charity for all, with firmness in the right, as God gives us to see the right, let us strive on to finish the work we are in; to bind up the nation's wounds, to care for him who shall have born the battle. And for his widow, and his orphan, -- to do all which may achieve and cherish a lasting peace among ourselves and with all nations."

Amen!

ABOUT THE AUTHOR

After a sixty year career as writer-director of many award-winning films and television programs Norman Weissman has written six novels and a memoir. Determined to oppose the silence in which lies become history, the author makes his reply in art to tell all of what he has witnessed.

He lives in Brookline Massachusetts with his wife Eveline.

www.ingramcontent.com/pod-product-compliance
Lightning Source LLC
Chambersburg PA
CBHW032148040426
42449CB00005B/445